Men Viewing Women as Art Objects

Studies in German Literature, Linguistics, and Culture

Edited by James Hardin
(*South Carolina*)

Die Fermate *by Erdmann Hummel,*
Neue Pinakothek, Munich. Courtesy of
Bayerische Staatsgemäldesammlungen.

Christoph E. Schweitzer

Men Viewing Women as Art Objects:
Studies in German Literature

CAMDEN HOUSE

Copyright © 1998 Christoph E. Schweitzer

All Rights Reserved. Except as permitted under current legislation,
no part of this work may be photocopied, stored in a retrieval system,
published, performed in public, adapted, broadcast, transmitted,
recorded, or reproduced in any form or by any means,
without the prior permission of the copyright owner.

First published 1998
Camden House
Drawer 2025
Columbia, SC 29202–2025 USA

Camden House is an imprint of Boydell & Brewer Inc.
PO Box 41026, Rochester, NY 14604–4126 USA
and of Boydell & Brewer Limited
PO Box 9, Woodbridge, Suffolk IP12 3DF, UK

ISBN: 1–57113–259–7

Library of Congress Cataloging-in-Publication Data

Schweitzer, Christoph E., 1922-
    Men viewing women as art objects : studies in German literature /
Christoph E. Schweitzer.
        p.   cm. – (Studies in German literature, linguistics, and
culture)
    Includes bibliographical references and index.
    ISBN 1–57113–259–7 (alk. paper)
    1. German literature – History and criticism. 2. Women in
literature. 3. Art in literature. 4. Women in art. 5. Art and
literature. 6. Man – woman relationships in literature. I. Title.
II. Series: Studies in German literature, linguistics, and culture
(Unnumbered)
PT151.W7S39 1998
830.9'352042—dc21   97–46706
                                                                       CIP

This publication is printed on acid-free paper.
Printed in the United States of America

For Cathy

Contents

Preface	xi
Introduction	1

1: The Female Portrait as a Spur to Possession

Turandot	5
Lessing: *Emilia Galotti*	8
Schikaneder / Mozart: *Die Zauberflöte*	11
Schiller: *Maria Stuart*	14

2: Possession of a Woman by Design

Goethe: *Die Leiden des jungen Werthers*	23
Lenz: *Der Waldbruder*	25
Plenzdorf: *Die neuen Leiden des jungen W.*	28
Goethe: *Der Triumph der Empfindsamkeit*	29
Dorothea Schlegel: *Florentin*	32
Fanny Lewald: *Jenny*	35
Thomas Mann: *Felix Krull*	37

3: Prophetic Vision

Goethe: *Wilhelm Meisters Lehrjahre*	44
Mörike: *Maler Nolten*	49

4: Seeing and Not Seeing: The Visual Image as Displacement

Hauff: *Die Bettlerin vom Pont des Arts*	57
Jensen: *Gradiva. Ein pompejanisches Phantasiestück*	61
Schimmang: *Intimität oder das Mädchen mit dem Perlengehänge*	65

5: The Painting as Transgression of Time and Space Boundaries

Nossack: *Dorothea*	68

6: Seeing and Enlightenment
    E. T. A. Hoffmann: *Die Fermate*   72
    Stifter: *Der Nachsommer*   77

7: Retrospective Vision: Closing the Circle
    Storm: *Immensee*   83

8: The Choice of Art Object   89

Conclusion   95

Select Bibliography   99

Index   101

Preface

This book has taken a long time. I first came across the significance of a painting in a work of German literature when I was still at Yale University. The function of the "Painting of the Sick Prince" within Goethe's *Wilhelm Meister* was the subject of an article that appeared in *PMLA* in 1957.[1] In the course of the years I found a great number of additional texts in which art objects played a major role, and I have published in the meantime the results of two of my findings. At one point it seemed best to me to present my findings in the form of a survey by type, in which the position of the work of art within the structure of the text would form the focus of the study. When readers of the manuscript did not think that a typological survey formed a cohesive whole, I looked at the material again and found the focus that I hope will give this book the desirable unity.

The topic of the relationship between literature and the visual arts is a vast one. This is not the place to review the many possible approaches to the study of the relationship. Suffice it to say that in the excellent survey by Ulrich Weisstein bearing the title "Literature and the Visual Arts," my approach belongs to category eight: "Literary works concerned with art and artists, whether real or imagined."[2] Within the specific category, I have chosen to investigate the different ways male characters in a literary text look at works of art depicting women, how that gaze comes about, and what its consequences are.

I will start with the most obvious example, the one in which the man looks at the portrait of a woman, is overwhelmed by her beauty, and rushes to conquer her. Within the Western tradition the story of Turandot, the name of the princess of a Persian tale, is the best known version among many in which the portrait of a woman exerts irresistible attraction for a man. Equally interesting is the situation in which a male character draws or obtains the portrait of a woman and in which that possession seems to give him a certain power over her. Actually, the most carefully worked out incident of this type is found in an American novel, in Mary McCarthy's *A Charmed Life*. During the protagonist's second marriage her portrait is acquired by her first husband. That purchase precedes a sexual encounter between the two. In film, one cannot help but think of the justly famous Otto Preminger film *Laura* (1944), in which detective Mark McPherson (Dana Andrews) literally falls in love with the portrait of the presumably deceased Gene Tierney.

The table of contents will give an indication of many other possibilities that authors have pursued when introducing a painting or a sculpture depicting a woman and a man looking at and then reacting to that work of art.

I could not include Mary McCarthy's *A Charmed Life* in the chapter I entitled "Possession of the Woman by Design" because I have limited my study to one literary tradition. And even within German literature I have undoubtedly overlooked many pertinent texts. The study is not meant to be exhaustive; rather, it is meant to introduce the reader to what I believe to be an original way of looking at literature and in so doing provide new insights into certain works.

There have been two studies with a similar focus to mine: Adolf Haslinger reports in a long article on paintings that have an important role in German Baroque novels and then mentions the occurrence of the phenomenon in later literature in a rather cursory manner.[3] In his important book, entitled *Erzählte Bilder* [Narrated Pictures], Bernard Dieterle takes up a great many works from both German and French literature and discusses a few of the same texts I have also chosen for my study. Dieterle emphasizes the way authors have integrated paintings of any kind into the narrative.[4] I will refer to his observations in connection with specific works. In addition, there are investigations of specific texts but there is no study that analyzes in a systematic way the topic I have chosen, that is, men looking at women as art objects. One recent study seemed to come close to my own, Wendy Lesser's *His Other Half. Men Looking at Women Through Art*. However, Lesser's "subject is man's relationship to the feminine — and, in this case, the way that relationship comes out in works of art."[5] Thus, her goal is basically different from mine in that she is investigating the way men look at women by analyzing art, created by men, art that depicts women.

The great number of works taken up as well as the interdisciplinary nature of the study make it difficult to do justice to every critical assessment of the specific text I have chosen. I believe, however, that

I have taken into consideration the most important, pertinent criticism in each case.

It must be kept in mind that the focus of the individual interpretations is not on the art object referred to in the text but on the use the author makes of it. Even in the case of those art works that are identified by the author and where we can verify their existence outside of the text, I purposefully have refrained from investigating their place in the history of art. Also, I do not pursue an author's evaluation of various artists and their works. These issues have nothing to do with an appreciation of the literary texts and how the art object depicting a woman influences a man's actions or thoughts. It is precisely the variety of possible interconnections between the work of art and a male character that is at the center of my study. It will be seen that the relationship between the art works depicting women and the various male characters is developed in many different ways and often with impressive artistry.

The initial research for this study was done in Berlin where I spent a sabbatical year granted by Bryn Mawr College in 1965–66. A one-semester fellowship at the Humanities Center at the University of North Carolina at Chapel Hill in the spring of 1991 with a reduced teaching load let me find the theme that provides the common link for the various chapters.

All translations are my own; the translations of shorter passages follow immediately after the German text; those of longer ones will be found in the endnotes at the end of each chapter.

C. E. S.
January 1998

Notes

[1] Christoph E. Schweitzer, "Wilhelm Meister und das Bild vom kranken Königssohn," *PMLA* 72 (1957), 419–32.

[2] In: *Interrelations of Literature*, ed. By Jean-Pierre Barricelli and Joseph Gibaldi (New York: The Modern Language Association of America, 1982), 251–77.

[3] Adolf Haslinger, "'Dies Bildnisz ist bezaubernd schön.' Zum Thema 'Motiv und epische Struktur' im höfischen Roman des Barock," *Literaturwissenschaftliches Jahrbuch*, NF, 9 (1968), 83–140.

[4] Bernard Dieterle, *Erzählte Bilder. Zum narrativen Umgang mit Gemälden* (Marburg: Hitzeroth, 1988).

[5] Wendy Lesser, *His Other Half. Men Looking at Women Through Art* (Cambridge, MA; London, England: Harvard UP, 1991), 4.

Introduction

Any study that deals, as this one does, with the interrelationship between literature and the visual arts should start with a short review of Gotthold Ephraim Lessing's *Laokoon: Oder über die Grenzen der Mahlerei und Poesie* [1766; Laocoon or on the Boundaries between Painting and Poetry]. Of special interest for the topic of this book are those issues raised by Lessing that pertain to the contrastive analysis of literature and the visual arts.

The Laocoon statue was discovered in 1506 and was immediately hailed as one of the greatest examples of classical art. It was praised in poems, copied, and imitated widely; it also has served as an inspiration for sculptors and painters until this day. In 1755 Johann Joachim Winckelmann published *Gedancken über die Nachahmung der Griechischen Wercke in der Mahlerei und Bildhauer-Kunst* [Thoughts on the Imitation of Greek Works in Painting and Sculpture] in which he extols the Laocoon group. He singles out the composed attitude of the priest, who, in spite of great pain, does not yell but controls his emotions and only groans. Winckelmann explains that in this way the Greek artist, who for him is also a philosopher, shows the priest's greatness in accordance with "noble simplicity, quiet grandeur" ("edle Einfalt, stille Größe"), Winckelmann's famous phrase. In other words, Winckelmann sees in the Laocoon group an example of stoicism.

Lessing's reaction came in 1766 with *Laocoon: Oder über die Grenzen der Mahlerei und Poesie*. We know now that much of what Lessing had to say in the essay had been stated previously by others. Still, it is his accomplishment to have brought together the various ideas and to have presented them as a coherent whole with exemplary clarity, at least as far as the main issues are concerned. These issues have been discussed ever since the publication of the essay.

Lessing shares Winckelmann's high opinion of the Laocoon group. However, he differs from Winckelmann when it comes to an explanation of the fact that Laocoon's mouth is only half open. Winckelmann, as I mentioned above, maintained that ethical reasons had led the artist to show us a person in control of his anguish. He does not, therefore, have his mouth wide open to cry out loud. Rather, he suppresses his pain and his despair to such a degree that he only groans. Lessing, on the other hand, points out that many Greek heroes exhibit extreme, uncontrolled emotions, in the Homeric epics as well as in dramas. Rather, Lessing argues, a wide-open mouth would have the effect of extreme ugliness. Beauty, however, is the aim of classical art. There is another equally important reason for the sculptor to have depicted Laocoon with his mouth only half open, and that reason is especially pertinent to what concerns me here. The sculptor selected the particular moment in the Laocoon story that immediately precedes its climax, that is, his and his two sons' deaths. Lessing calls it the "pregnant" moment, the one that lets the imagination of the viewer supply what is to follow. Our imaginative power surpasses anything the artist could have depicted precisely because our imagination is not limited by material and spatial constraints. It follows, that, in addition to giving an ugly expression permanence, the wide-open mouth would have meant that the viewer could only have imagined a let-down of the tension depicted in the Laocoon group.

Lessing has thus arrived at several generalizations about the difference between the visual arts (painting and sculpture) and poetry (he has epic poetry and drama in mind). Extreme emotions accompanying the climax of an action can be the subject of epic poetry and of drama because they form part of a sequence of mental images for the reader. Such emotions should, on the other hand, not be shown in the visual arts because their representation means ugliness instead of beauty and inhibits the creative power of the viewer's imagination. Furthermore, while the visual arts can only depict one moment in time, poetry means sequence of time since words follow one another. The proper mode for the sculptor and painter is therefore simultaneity while it is action for the author. Both art forms, though, can suggest the other mode: the sculptor and painter can suggest previous, and, more important, subsequent events as I pointed out above in the discussion of the pregnant moment. The literary artist in turn can suggest simultaneity, for example by the use of adjectives. Basically, though, poetry means passage of time. Therefore, it cannot successfully attempt description, that is, express a moment in time. An author trying to describe in detail a scene at a given moment or the looks of a person would be in danger of losing the reader who relates literature to the development of action.

There is one more generalization in Lessing's *Laokoon* essay that is relevant to the issue of this book, the discussion of how the representation of beauty can be achieved. There is, of course, no problem for the sculptor or painter who can give direct expression to beauty. An author, on the other hand, is according to Lessing's dictum kept from describing in any detail let us say a beautiful woman. Basing his argument on Homer as he does frequently, Lessing posits that it is the effect of beauty that convinces the reader that the person or object must indeed be beautiful. The well-known prototype for Lessing's assertion is the scene in which the ancient Trojans, who have lost sons and relatives fighting the Greeks on account of Helen, forgive her when they look at her. Lessing himself was to use the technique most effectively in *Emilia Galotti*, a drama I will take up in the first chapter. In that play the protagonist is in no way described — there is one reference to the color of her hair — but still she is in the reader's mind clearly the most beautiful woman imaginable. We know that Emilia is so beautiful on the basis of the effect she has on many characters of the play, with two male figures trying to make her their possession and one of them losing his life in the process.

The focus of my book is on the interpretation of a number of works of German literature in which a woman is represented in a painting or as a sculpture and a man reacts to the painting or sculpture. The types of reaction I have discovered form the various chapters. That in the western tradition it is the male who is attracted to the female, often on the basis of her looks, at least initially, is a generally accepted phenomenon. The social psychologist David M. Buss reports that the phenomenon can be observed even on a world-wide basis: "As in our American college population, men throughout the world placed a high value on physical attractiveness in a partner."[1]

The issue of the importance of female beauty for men is, of course, very much debated today. Innumerable literary texts reflect, at least since medieval times, the stereotypical phenomenon of the male's eye spotting the female and the ensuing erotic attraction exerted by the female on the male. Movies and television offer just as many incidents where the relationship between the sexes is established when the male character sees a woman for the first time and is immediately "taken" by her even though he doesn't know anything about her character, the so-called "love at first sight." Perhaps in the future, literature will reflect cases in which the woman, after seeing a man for the first time, takes the initiative. There might already exist texts that show such female initiative. However, my readings in German literature have indicated that even in the case of women authors the male is the one looking at the woman, whether as character in the text or as portrayed in art or as both. The many ways such viewing of a woman as art is developed into a story or a drama is the theme of this study.

Notes

[1] "The Strategies of Human Mating," *American Scientist* 82 (1994), 238–249, here 245.

1: The Female Portrait as a Spur to Possession

Turandot

When Fröben, the male protagonist of Wilhelm Hauff's *Die Bettlerin vom Pont des Arts* (The Beggar Woman of the Pont des Arts), spends day after day looking at the portrait of a woman in a Stuttgart gallery, the people who have observed his strange behavior think: "Am Ende ist er wohl in das Bild verliebt (. . .), wie Kalaf in das der Prinzessin Turandot" [It must be that he is in love with the picture (. . .) as Kalaf is in love with the picture of Princess Turandot].[1] Hauff thus sees in the story of Turandot the archetype of a man's desire for a woman, spurred on by the sight of her picture. Hauff had most likely Schiller's *Turandot, Prinzessin von China. Ein tragikomisches Märchen nach Gozzi* [Turandot, Princess of China. A tragic-comic Fairy Tale after Gozzi] in mind when he had the town people make the comparison between Fröben and Kalaf. Schiller's *Turandot* is based, as the subtitle states, on the German translation of Carlo Gozzi's play *Turandot, fiaba chinese teatrale tragicomica* of 1762. Gozzi, in turn, has as his source a French translation of an Arabian story that exists in many different versions. Rather than trying to account for the various versions, I want to show, in connection with the earliest text in which the motif comes up, how the portrait of the woman functions as the incentive for the man to try to conquer her.[2]

The earliest and best text for my purpose is by the Persian poet known as Nizami who died ca. 1200, shortly after having completed the Romantic epos *The Seven Pictures (Haft Paykar)*.[3] The central part of the epos, "The Seven Princesses," contains the story that concerns me here. It is "The Story Told by the Russian Princess on Tuesday in the Red Pavilion of Mars" in which, after a short introductory section, the princess is asked by King Bahram to tell "The Story of Turandot's Riddles." Actually, the name Turandot is not in the original but was supplied by the translator because of the subsequent association in later versions of the story with the name Turandot as its main character. As is evident from the above, there is a very intricate set of frames, characteristic of oriental literature. Of special interest here is the outer frame for "The Seven Princesses." The frame tells about King Bahram, who, when still a prince, notices a locked room, has it opened, discovers on the walls the portraits of seven princesses and one of himself among them. Also, there are words to the effect that, when he is king, he should ask the fathers of the seven princesses to give their consent that he may ask their daughters to marry him. Once upon the throne, he obtains the consent and builds for each of the seven a pavilion, each one decorated in a different color. The outer frame, thus, is closely related to the theme of the story told by the Russian princess in that a man chances upon the portraits of women and upon words that tell him the conditions he must fulfill to be able to marry them.[4]

According to "The Story of Turandot's Riddles" the protagonist is as beautiful as she is intelligent. She does not think that any man is worthy of her and thus causes her father great anguish since the rejected suitors turn to him to change his daughter's mind. She finally asks her father that a castle be built on a mountain where she is known as "The Lady of the Mountain Fortress." The path leading to the castle has on both sides mechanical guards of her own design, guards that prove deadly to anyone who does not know their secret. Also, the gate to the inside of the castle is invisible. Turandot is not only beautiful and possesses great scientific and magical knowledge, she is also an accomplished painter who paints her own life-size portrait which she has hung on the nearby city gate. Next to it she has a sign that explains the four conditions any suitor must fulfill before she will consent to marry him. They are: be of noble birth, get through the path to the castle proper, find the gate and solve the riddles. Dozens of men come to see the portrait even though they were warned not to do so. They say they just want to look at the picture of the princess. But as soon as they have seen her portrait, they are mesmerized by her beauty and rush to conquer her only to lose their lives in the process, their skulls then being placed next to her portrait. Finally, a courageous, intelligent, and handsome prince happens to come to the city where her portrait hangs next to the many skulls of the unsuccessful suitors. He is as much overwhelmed by her beauty and a desire to possess her as all the other suitors but he also considers the fate of these predecessors. His state of mind is described as that of a person stricken with an incurable disease. He realizes, though, that there is a poisonous viper hidden behind the beautiful exterior. Thus there is a struggle between his passionate and his rational sides while he looks at her portrait day after day. He then decides to search out a wise man who lives in an isolated area, and, after having spent a long time with him, succeeds in entering the castle. Turandot, in spite of being attracted to him when she first sees him and in spite of her father's plea to end the test right then, has the prince submit to her riddles which he resolves brilliantly.

It is interesting to note that the prince has the skulls of the unsuccessful suitors interred and Turandot's portrait taken down for safekeeping even before he has solved the riddles. He is obviously already so confident that he will be victorious that he disposes of her double, her portrait. In this version of the Turandot story her seemingly contradictory attitude toward men is especially obvious: on the one hand she looks down on all of them as being mentally her inferior but on the other she entices men to conquer her by painting a portrait of herself, obviously a portrait of special charm so that men lose their heads over her beauty. But Turandot is also conscious of what constitutes the right man for her: he must not only want to risk his life for her sake but also must be intelligent and circumspect. Both she and the prince thus prepare for each other so that sensuousness and maturity meet to form an ideal union.

For the purpose of this study it is important to see that all the unsuccessful suitors as well as the successful one are first attracted to Turandot on the basis of her portrait. Every one of them is immediately overcome with passionate desire for her even though he has as yet not spoken a word with her and even though he is aware of the cruelty of her nature. The visual signal is crucial then in this case, and Turandot knows that that aspect arouses the male's desire and compels him to action. However, she is wise enough to insure that the man whom she is willing to marry is not only physically attracted to her but also has the intelligence to match hers and, by the type of riddles posed to him, the empathy necessary to respond to the symbolic language of her beautiful riddles.

Lessing: *Emilia Galotti*

Gotthold Ephraim Lessing's *Emilia Galotti* (1772) is the first important work of German literature in which the portrait of a woman plays a crucial role. Still, I hesitated to include *Emilia Galotti* in this section since technically neither portrait — there are two in the play — provides the first stimulus for a man to try to conquer the woman depicted. The Prince, the man involved here, has known both women whose portraits he is shown at the beginning of the play. The reason for my including Lessing's tragedy here after all is based on the fact that the scene with Emilia's portrait serves, while not initiating the action, almost the same function as the portrait of Turandot in that Emilia's portrait intensifies sharply the already strong erotic attraction she has exerted on the Prince. In addition, the scene in which the two portraits are shown to him by Conti, the court painter, has had a noticeable effect on later playwrights, especially Schiller whose *Maria Stuart* I will discuss later. Also of special interest in *Emilia Galotti* is the doubling of the women portrayed, bringing about rather different reactions in the man looking at the paintings.[5]

Hettore Gonzaga, Prince of Guastalla — referred to in the play and in the secondary literature as the Prince — wakes up early on the day of the action since his infatuation with the beautiful Emilia does not let him sleep long. He had met her and briefly spoken to her at a recent soirée, but had since only watched her from a distance when she worshipped in one of the local churches. The morning of the beginning of the play he is given a letter from his erstwhile paramour, Countess Orsina. We learn subsequently that she is asking the Prince to meet with her later on that day. Since Emilia has replaced Orsina, the Prince puts the letter away without so much as bothering to read it. Then comes Orsina's second attempt to rekindle his affection for her. She has sent Conti to the Prince to show him a portrait of herself that the Prince had commissioned when they were still lovers. It is, as the Prince, no longer in love with her, observes, extremely flattering. Had he still been in love, he would of course not have had such a sober, reflective way of judging what the painter had accomplished. His emotional distance to the person depicted lets him detect the artist's technique of embellishing Orsina's features. Thus, while she counts on the effect the portrait of a beautiful woman is supposed to have on a man, the Prince does not react in the hoped-for manner since emotionally he is committed in a different direction.

Conti also brings along Emilia's portrait because he is proud of having painted such a beautiful woman. The painting had been commissioned by her father, in connection with Emilia's impending marriage. Conti had made a copy that he wants to show the Prince. Both the Prince and the audience are kept in suspense as to the identity of the woman of the second painting. The Prince, assuming that she is probably Conti's beloved and about to dismiss the second portrait as being obviously inferior to the ideal that he harbors in his heart, is taken aback when he discovers that it is of Emilia. At first the Prince thinks that the portrait must be a figment of his imagination. In the ensuing dialogue between the Prince and Conti the Prince has a difficult time in trying to give his infatuation with Emilia a reasonable appearance. Conti's praise of her exceptional beauty and his disquisitions on the limitations of his art in face of such beauty and on other matters concerning painting and painters, fall on deaf ears since the Prince is completely absorbed with Emilia, that is, with her portrait. As the painter observes, his whole being is in his eyes, and he is willing to pay for the portrait any amount Conti might ask. The painter is fully aware that it is the subject matter of his art that the Prince is buying not the artistry that went into the portrait.

Orsina's painting Conti is to take back, and the Prince corrects himself as he does so often when his emotional, subconscious side is about to take over and make him say something like "and hide it some place, I don't ever want to see it again" or a more indecent version of that sentiment. The Prince catches himself though and has Conti order a frame for Orsina's portrait so that it can be hung in one of the castle's picture galleries. Emilia's portrait the Prince obviously wants to keep with him, at any price. Conti is perfectly correct in sensing that it is Emilia herself whom the Prince would love to buy, at any price. As he says in the monologue of the fifth scene of the first act: "Am liebsten kauft' ich dich, Zauberin, von dir selbst!" [What I would love best is to buy you, you enchantress, from you yourself!] We will come across the supposedly bewitching quality of the woman desired again later in this section. Here I want to point out the parallel between the Prince's buying Emilia's portrait and thus hoping to have bought her herself and Martha's ex-husband buying her portrait in Mary McCarthy's *A Charmed Life*. In contrast to Lessing's play in which the Prince is denied the "possession" of the real Emilia, in McCarthy's novel the purchase leads to the seduction of the ex-wife. The mercantile language used here by both the Prince and Martha's ex-husband finds its exact parallel in Margo Wilson's and Martin Daly's "The Man Who Mistook His Wife for a Chattel" when they write that

> men lay claim to particular women as songbirds lay claim to territories, as lions lay claim to kill, or as people of both sexes lay claim to valuables [. . .] referring to man's view of women as "proprietary" is more than a metaphor: Some of the same mental algorithms are apparently activated in the marital and mercantile sphere.[6]

After his purchase of the portrait the Prince treats it as if it were Emilia herself. He would love to spend the morning alone with "Emilia," and when Marinelli, his chamberlain, comes in, turns the face of her portrait toward the wall since he is too jealous to share "her" with anyone else.[7] After learning that Emilia Galotti is getting married that very day, he throws it to the ground in desperation. When Marinelli subsequently comes up with the promise to try to get the marriage postponed and the Prince has given Marinelli *carte blanche* to proceed with whatever plans he might have, the Prince sees a tiny ray of hope, lifts the portrait from the floor but cannot bring himself to look at Emilia since that would be too painful.

The rest of the play does not contain any further reference to either one of the portraits. The sight of Emilia's portrait, then, "unleashes a veritable paroxysm of self-indulgent, lustful, impulsive, irresponsible, and ultimately murderous behavior on the part of the Prince," as Neill Flax puts it.[8]

Emilia's portrait serves one additional function in the play. It expresses symbolically the outcome between Odoardo, Emilia's father, and his antagonist, the Prince. In the end the father will be the one to reclaim the daughter from the Prince by killing her. He possesses the original portrait while the Prince had only bought a copy.

Anyone looking at the way Lessing brings out Emilia's beauty must immediately observe that he follows here his own principles as developed in *Laokoon* which he had completed just six years prior to the drama. Beauty is made evident in literature by showing its effect, in this case the beautiful Emila's effect on a number of men. In the next sections I will take up two more works in which the portrait of a woman spurs on a man to conquer her and then conclude with some general comments on how the authors of the works taken up in this chapter have handled the introduction of paintings of women into the plots.

Schikaneder / Mozart: *Die Zauberflöte*

In German literature the first text I have come across to contain the use of the portrait of a woman to entice a man to pursue her is Emanuel Schikaneder's *Die Zauberflöte* [1790; The Magic Flute]. Few operas are as much shrouded in legend and hypothesis as to sources and even as to the authorship of the libretto as *Die Zauberflöte*. But for my purpose it suffices to know that much of the content of the opera is based on a collection of tales by Christoph Martin Wieland entitled *Dschinnistan* (1786–89). As the title indicates, the origin of many of the stories goes back to the east and thus to the same area from where the Turandot theme came from.

Here is how Schikaneder introduces Pamina's portrait. Her mother, the Queen of the Night, has lost Pamina to Sarastro who also has the symbol of power, the solar circle (*Sonnenkreis*) which was given to him by Pamina's father before his death. When Tamino, a prince, happens upon the temple of the Queen of the Night, he is at the mercy of a snake since he has no arrow left in his bow and he swoons. Three ladies come to his rescue by killing the snake. When they discover how beautiful he is they conclude he might be the one to liberate Pamina from Sarastro's domain and return her to the Queen of the Night. They report the incident to the Queen who has them show Tamino her daughter's portrait with the explanation that, if he were to be attracted to her and if he were to rescue her, he would have happiness, honor, and fame. In other words, he could marry her. This means of course that Pamina is being disposed of, unbeknownst to her, purely on the basis of her looks that are to be the incentive to Tamino to risk his life for her. We can also see that the Queen of the Night is fully aware of the connection between a man's looking at female beauty and his subsequent erotic desire and impetus to conquest. In the case of Turandot it was she herself who thus enticed men, here it is the mother. Both Turandot's and the Queen of the Night's calculations prove correct. Upon seeing the picture, the two men rush to conquer the woman depicted, fully aware of the extreme dangers involved in the undertaking. One should probably add here that such dangers actually enhance the woman's attractiveness for the man so challenged, since overcoming them would in his opinion prove not only his manliness in her eyes but would also make him assume that she would have to yield to him.

Tamino reacts, then, in the anticipated manner. He first looks at the portrait with interest, then falls deeper and deeper in love with the woman depicted, and is oblivious to what is going on around him, a reminiscence of the Prince's absorption with Emilia's portrait in Lessing's *Emilia Galotti*. Tamino's aria at this point — like so much else of the opera — has become famous:

> Dies Bildniß ist bezaubernd schön,
> Wie noch kein Auge je geseh'n!
> Ich fühl' es, wie dies Götterbild
> Mein Herz mit neuer Regung füllt.
> Dieß Etwas kann ich zwar nicht nennen,
> Doch fühl' ichs hier wie Feuer brennen.
> Soll *die* Emfindung Liebe seyn?
> Ja, ja! die Liebe ist's allein.
> O wenn ich sie nur finden könnte!
> O wenn sie doch schon vor mir stände!
> Ich würde — würde — warm und rein —
> Was würde ich! — Sie voll Enzücken
> An diesen heißen Busen drücken,
> Und ewig wäre sie dann mein.[9]

Mozart's music with its tender appogiaturas and pulsations underlines Tamino's words that express astonishment at Pamina's beauty and his racing heart. For my purpose the word "bezaubernd" is significant in that it points to the magical power exerted by what the man sees and to the many cognates and associations that the word entails: bewitching, mesmerizing, enchanting. The woman as sorceress is, of course, a common occurrence in literature, a way of describing the involuntary arousal of the "right" man's erotic desire. Tamino, then, is thus aroused by the sight of Pamina's portrait and would, if he were able to find her, would ... Here he begins to stutter since he doesn't dare say "have her" as the less inhibited Prince puts it in Lessing's play when looking at Emilia's portrait.

Tamino ends the aria by saying that he would press Pamina to his bosom.

Pamina's portrait and its effect on Tamino are also discussed by David Freedberg in a chapter that has a similar focus to mine and is entitled "Arousal by Image." Freedberg stresses the movement in Tamino's imagination "from beautiful picture to the beautiful woman represented on it" and Tamino's subsequently being "overwhelmed with a sense of her potential presence, her potential liveliness." I fully agree with Freedberg but find that he does not see the erotic arousal that Tamino experiences when looking at Pamina's portrait.[10] After all, there is the sensation of a "burning fire" of line six of the aria, Tamino mentions his "heißen Busen" (line 13), being both "warm und rein" (line 11), and there is the hesitation when trying to express what he would do if she were to stand in front of him. His final words that he would press her to his bosom are clearly a polite circumlocution for his wish to sleep with her. Before being able to do that he must first pass various tests Sarastro and his men have devised for both Pamina and Tamino.

The Queen of the Night has overheard every word of Tamino's confession of love and now tells him that her daughter has been taken away from her and that she is in the hands of an evil spirit (Dämon), meaning Sarastro. What follows, as is well known, is Tamino's successful "rescue" of Pamina from Sarastro who turns out to be a most benevolent, enlightened, and idealized high priest. He is the spiritual center of a group of men who in a Freemason-like manner and with all the trappings of that and other similar societies presides over the rites, and, what is of concern to me here, specifically over the rites of initiation. Both Pamina and Tamino have to undergo a long series of difficult and often dangerous tests that both, of course, pass brilliantly. By including Pamina, who, as love personified, leads Tamino through the various terrifying entrances ("Schreckenspforten"), Schikaneder and Mozart add women to the male-centered Freemasons. Both emerge victorious from the various tests in priestly garments.[11] Thus, similar to what we observed in the case of Turandot, both Pamina and Tamino can get together as equals only after having gone through many trials and tribulations. She has to prove her ability to resist attempted rape and then show her courage in the face of danger, while he has to show his fortitude and steadfastness and in so doing and in being together with Pamina and in admiring her courage converts his initial infatuation with her looks and his erotic desire into an attraction to her as a full person.

Die Zauberflöte would not have had the success it has enjoyed for over two centuries if it were not for Papageno's role in the opera. Schikaneder, who sang Papageno when the opera was first performed, created in the Papageno/Papagena pair a wonderfully humorous counterpart to the heavy moralizing of Sarastro and his men and the equally serious nature of Pamina's and Tamino's love language. Schikaneder, among other ingenious ideas, has Papageno enter Sarastro's realm ahead of Tamino and has him take along Pamina's portrait so as to be able to identify Pamina. It will serve her as proof that Papageno was indeed sent by her mother. But before she has time to reflect on the origin of this portrait, when Papageno first sees Pamina and he has heard that she is the daughter of the Queen of the Night, he looks at her portrait and compares its features — color of the eyes, lips, and hair — with those of the Pamina in front of him so as to verify that she is indeed Pamina. To add to the humor of the naïve comparison — the features compared could be the same in many women — Papageno, while satisfied in general with the result of the comparison, cannot understand why the Pamina in front of him has hands and feet while on her portrait she lacks both.

Schiller: *Maria Stuart*

Schiller uses paintings already in his first play, *Die Räuber* [1781; The Robbers]. Karl Moor, disguised as a stranger and assumed to have been killed during the battle of Prague, visits his father's castle. There he talks to his adored Amalia who, when they walk through the portrait gallery and stand in front of his portrait, cannot hide her tears. Thus, Karl knows that she still loves him. In *Die Verschwörung des Fiesco zu Genua* [1783; The Conspiracy of Fiesco in Genoa] the conspirators try to find out Fiesco's commitment to their cause by having him react to a painting depicting the scene in which Virginia's father is about to stab his daughter in front of Appius Claudius who claimed her as a slave. In other words, a scene from the same event in Roman history that Lessing used as the basis for *Emilia Galotti*. The test as such does not have the results anticipated, since Fiesco admires the way the artist has brought out Virginia's beauty and does not reveal clearly where his political sentiments lie. Schiller obviously wanted to show Fiesco as a character who is, at least at this point of the play, not dominated by erotic desires but carefully calculates every step of his actions and is in complete control of his emotions. Fiesco then throws the painting to the ground and declares that he has already initiated the action to overthrow the tyrant not just painted such action, as the artist had. He refers here to the fact that after Virginia's death the Romans staged a successful rebellion.

Schiller's *Der Geisterseher* [1787–89; The Ghost Seer] describes in detail the intricate and elaborate means that bring about first the spiritual and material ruination of a Protestant Prince and then his conversion to Catholicism. The various ways of achieving the desired goal are masterfully devised by an Armenian whom Schiller wisely keeps in the background. At one point the Armenian wants to have a woman participate in his scheme and commissions an artist to paint three different types of women, a Madonna, an Héloise, and an almost naked Venus. All three are of exceptional beauty and the paintings of exactly the same value. Still, the prince immediately chooses the painting of the Madonna and is willing to pay a large sum for it. But the painter — instructed of course by the Armenian — demands that the Prince buy all three portraits. Before the Prince can come to a resolution about that condition, the three paintings disappear. He is then enticed to visit a certain church; inside, he is by himself when to his amazement he discovers a female figure made visible by the single beam of the evening sun. When the Prince has come to this point of his story — which he is telling to the narrator — the latter asks the Prince whether the apparition of the woman was something real and not just a painting or a figment of his imagination. Similarly, the Prince in *Emilia Galotti*, when first seeing Emilia's portrait, believes that she must be a figment of his imagination. In *Der Geisterseher* the Prince gives a detailed description of the woman who is supposedly so much absorbed in her prayers that she does not notice him. Again, we have here evidence of the careful coaching by the Armenian and his men. The woman involved is of course the model for the painter's Madonna the Prince had chosen among the three paintings shown to him earlier. The painting of a woman is used in *Der Geisterseher*, then, to find out a man's erotic preference, then make him fall in love with the woman portrayed and thus make him dependent on that woman. As in the case of *Fiesco*, the painting is used as a psychological test and the scheme has the intended result, in contrast to the earlier play. Except that the human guinea pig, the woman whose portrait the Prince wanted to buy and whom he meets, actually falls in love with him and has to be killed.

When we approach *Maria Stuart* (1800) with the use of the Madonna painting in *Der Geisterseher* in mind, we see an aspect that otherwise might very well appear as a chance encounter. In the first act of *Maria Stuart*, Mortimer, the nephew of the man at whose castle Maria Stuart is imprisoned, gives an account to her of his travel to Rome and his being overwhelmed by the beauty and splendor of the presence of the Catholic Church in the holy city. It is there that he converts to Catholicism. On the way back to England, in Reims, he is in the hands of Jesuits when he happens to come across a portrait of Maria. Thinking back to the Madonna painting in the novel and the role secret agents played in that work — in which, as in the play, a Protestant is converted to Catholicism — one cannot help but assume that that encounter between Mortimer and Maria's portrait was the result of clever manipulations on the part of the Jesuits whose reputation for intrigue and questionable machinations was well known to Schiller. In both the novel and the play the plan works. Mortimer, at the sight of Maria's portrait, is overwhelmed by her miraculous charm and so powerfully moved that his emotions make him speechless. He is then told about the fate of the Queen as seen from the Catholic point of view. When Mortimer learns that Maria has been transferred to his uncle's castle, he takes that as a sign from heaven that he is the one chosen to free the Queen. He is given instructions as to how to proceed and to act the loyal Englishman, a scheme he carries off so successfully that even his uncle and Queen Elizabeth are fooled, with the latter trying to have him secretly murder Maria. Just as Mortimer's conversion to Catholicism was the result of external, sensual impressions and not the result of a deep understanding of the Catholic faith, so his attempt to rescue Maria stems not so much from a conviction that this is what is morally and politically right but from a personal, erotic desire. That desire originated when he saw Maria's portrait in Reims. Interestingly enough, the Cardinal of Guise had told Mortimer that we must first *see* what our hearts are to believe in (lines 479–480), an assertion that fits Mortimer's case exactly. He again and again stresses the visual aspect of Maria's beauty as the reason for his rescue attempt: "Auferstehen würde Englands ganze Jugend,/ ... sähe / Der Brite seine

Königin!" to which Maria replies: "Wohl ihr / Sähe jeder Brite sie mit Euren Augen!" [lines 556–561; If an Englishman were to see his queen, all of England's youth would rise up . . . She would fare well if every Englishman were to see her with your eyes]. And a bit later Mortimer tells Maria that every time he comes to her quarters he is delighted to look at her.

    More than in Mortimer, Maria places her hopes of being freed in her old admirer Leicester who had forsaken her for Elizabeth. This was a calculated move on Leicester's part who is governed by selfish political ambition. And while he has gained the status of Queen Elizabeth's favorite, he suffers from her moods, her expectation of his slavish obedience to her every whim. In addition, Elizabeth is not in any way to be compared as to looks with Maria. The latter uses Mortimer as a messenger to carry a letter from her to Leicester pleading with him to rescue her. With the letter she sends him her portrait in the knowledge that he will more readily be moved to action by the erotic attraction that her beauty exerts than by any humanitarian or political consideration. Maria feels so strongly about the impact her portrait should have on Leicester that she reminds him of it in a second letter (line 2783). Similarly, Turandot had her self-portrait hung on public display so as to entice men to conquer her in her virginal fortress. And in a like manner, the Queen of the Night had used Pamina's portrait to prompt Tamino to free her daughter from what she claims were Sarastro's clutches. When Mortimer gives Leicester the letter Maria had written to him, he first looks at her portrait, kisses it, and then contemplates it in silent rapture. Only then does he scan the message. Leicester tells Mortimer that when he had been put down by Elizabeth's plans to marry the Duke of Anjou, his thoughts had turned back to Maria: "Mariens Bild in ihrer Reize Glanz, / Stand neu vor mir" [lines 1819–20; Maria's picture in the splendor of her charms stood freshly before me]. Again, her image, that is, her beauty, is the key aspect of her person that makes Leicester think of her. We also learn in the course of the discussion between Leicester and Mortimer that they assume that she will be expected to owe sexual favors to her rescuer. Even Maria herself conveys that much in her letter to Leicester in the hope that the combination of her portrait and the promise of sexual favors will spur him on to action. But, as Mortimer bitterly remarks, Leicester remains the opportunist and coward he has always been and is reluctant to get involved in Mortimer's rescue plan. The latter claims that, while he is only intent on freeing Maria, Leicester's aim is to "possess" her (line 1866). But this is obviously a lie, or at best a complete self-deception, since it is clear that Mortimer is just as eager to "possess" Maria as his attempted rape of Maria in scene four of act four shows.

Mortimer, the fanatic, commits suicide to prevent his being captured by Elizabeth's guards. His last words are addressed to his beloved Maria ("Geliebte!" line 2817) as well as to the Virgin Mary, thus giving once more testimony to the questionable juxtaposition in his drives of the sensual and the religious. In Schiller's play Maria's beauty, first conveyed to Mortimer through her portrait, is at the bottom of the tragic ending. His attempt to free and "possess" her precipitates her execution.

When we look back at the texts taken up in this chapter, we discover, first of all, that there is little or no description of any of the supposedly so beautiful women who are central to the various plots. While every reader will undoubtedly agree that Pamina and Maria, Queen of Scotland, and especially Turandot and Emilia Galotti must have been extraordinarily beautiful, the readers will not be able to say anything about the physical attributes of these women. We do not learn about the color of their eyes nor about their height or the shape of their noses. Clearly, each author has purposefully withheld any descriptive adjectives. One reason for the omission is obvious: had the author given us a specific type of female beauty, we would no longer be able to empathize with the power exerted by that woman over all men since our ideal will, by necessity, be different from the one described. However, the reader's identification with the male character's seeing in the woman pursued the epitome of beauty is essential for the success of these texts. There is also the problem with extended descriptive passages, as Lessing pointed out in *Laokoon* (chapter XX). Readers are not only bored normally but also usually unable to form an organic whole out of the various pieces of information supplied by the text. Such a whole is, according to Lessing, automatically supplied in a painting or a sculpture.

Again, we can turn to *Laokoon* to find the reason for our knowing that these women are so extraordinarily beautiful: it is based on the effect they have on men. Lessing refers in this connection to Helen in the *Iliad*, and Schiller has his Maria called a Helen, too (line 84).

As Lessing points out, there are the old Trojans whose sons have been killed because of Helen and who have all the reasons in the world to condemn her but who, when seeing her, forgive her. In Schiller's play it is old Talbot who grows enthusiastic and surrenders his rational judgment when thinking of Maria (II, 3). Beauty, then, is imagined in the mind of the reader by its effect: among the central women characters in the texts of this chapter Turandot and Emilia stand out in our mind as possessing unusual attractiveness. In *Die Zauberflöte* Pamina's portrait has the expected effect on Tamino but, except for the unfortunate Monostatos, we hear of no other man who was taken in by her beauty. The woman in *Der Geisterseher* is attractive to the Prince because she corresponds exactly to his ideal of a beautiful woman but again we do not hear of other men who react in the same way. The case of Turandot is a model for the type of effect Lessing has in mind. Men risk impossible odds to conquer her and do so in spite of the sight of the many skulls of the previous suitors. Emilia Galotti is so attractive that a nobleman is about to marry her even though this is a step that will exclude him from court society. The Prince's uncontrollable passion and the painter's unconditional praise of her beauty give evidence of how much she *must* be the ideal as to physical appearance. Maria, Queen of Scotland, too appears in the reader's eyes as being unusually beautiful on the same basis as Turandot: the list of executed would-be liberators is recited repeatedly as a warning to Mortimer, and, while we do not learn about their precise motivations for trying to rescue her, we assume, on the basis of what we know from Mortimer's case, that her beauty must have played a role in their attempts, too. There is a problem, though, as to Maria's beauty: many readers will know that historically she was old and arthritic at the time of her execution. Such knowledge might interfere with our accepting her as having the same overpowering beauty that Turandot and Emilia must have had. However, this possible interference does not exist for the spectator who sees only the actress on the stage.

    The four main texts discussed in this chapter contain plots that are characterized by abundant action. The action is initiated in key moments by a male who has seen the portrait of a woman and is driven to win her on the basis of her looks. The stimulus, then is purely physical. The various attempts to conquer the woman behind the portrait have as a result works that are full of action. Thus, these works agree perfectly with what Lessing has described as an essential aspect of every literary text, that is, events that follow one another in time, in contrast to the visual arts that are characterized by the depiction of one moment in time. To be sure, the works taken up in this chapter also make reference to paintings. However, their subject matters are never described in any detail; rather, it is the effect of the beauty of the woman portrayed that the four authors have brought out.

Finally, it is instructive to consider the relationship between the woman and the man after he has seen her portrait and has set out to win her. The clearest development in attitude on the part of the man is in *Turandot* and *Die Zauberflöte*. Turandot had dreaded marriage as the surest way for a woman to become a man's slave. She wants to remain free. Thus, she either has to remain single or has to prepare the conditions for a husband who would respect her as a person with her own rights. The prince, to be sure, is as enraptured by her looks as the other men who preceded him have been, but he seeks counsel before attempting to win her. In all his moves he shows himself to be what she had wanted in a man, to be a considerate person. As I mentioned above, both Pamina and Tamino have to undergo a lengthy initiation before they are allowed to become a pair. The Prince's attitude toward Emilia Galotti in Lessing's play doesn't change radically — after all, everything takes place in less than a day — but one can detect in him a sign of respect for Emilia once she has been brought to his castle. Basically, though, he does not and will not change in his views of women. Mortimer in Schiller's *Maria Stuart* deludes himself when he claims that he wants to reinstate Maria to the throne in which she, according to him and others, belongs. In reality he wants to possess Maria, the beautiful woman, to whose rescue he was spurred on by her portrait.

Notes

[1] Wilhelm Hauff, *Werke*, ed. Bernhard Zeller (Frankfurt/M: Insel, 2 vols, 1969), vol 1, 399.

² The best account of the Turandot topic in literature and opera I found in Elisabeth Frenzel's *Stoffe der Weltliteratur. Ein Lexikon dichtungsgeschichtlicher Längsschnitte* (Stuttgart: Kröner, 1983, sixth ed.), 767–71. However, the critical literature on "Turandot" is centered on the theme of the woman who refuses to marry and who has the many suitors who fail to solve the riddle or riddles she poses to them executed and their skulls put on public display. The theme of the portrait that arouses men's passion is mentioned at best in passing. Further references are found in J. Christoph Bürgel, "'Dies Bildnis ist bezaubernd schön.' Zum Motiv 'Love through sight of picture' in der klassischen Literatur des islamischen Orients," *Michael Stettler zum 70. Geburtstag. Von Angesicht zu Angesicht. Porträtstudien*, ed. Florens Deuchler, Mechthild Flury-Lemberg, Karel Otavsky (Bern: Stämpfli, 1983), 31–39.

³ I used the English version entitled *The Story of the Seven Princesses* (London: Bruno Cassirer, 1976).

⁴ There is a political fable by Jurek Becker entitled *Das Bild* [1980; The Painting] that forms part of a collection of stories *Nach der ersten Zukunft* (Frankfurt/M, Suhrkamp) and that contains an interesting variation of the motif of attaching a condition to obtaining the hand of a woman, in this case of a princess. The condition is that he who wants to marry the princess must first kill a dragon which devours a human being every day. The protagonist has her portrait and looks at it constantly but cannot muster the courage to go and fight the dragon for years. Standing at the window of his room one night, he again thinks of the terrible dragon, then switches on the light, and sees, to his horror, that the princess of the portrait has turned into an old woman with sunken cheeks, a wrinkled forehead, and despair in her eyes. He quickly turns out the light again. When, after a while, he turns it back on, the portrait shows again the beautiful princess with whom he had fallen in love. He finally comes to the realization that the princess must have, in contrast to her portrait, aged during all these years and that she must have become despondent over the fact that no one had come to kill the dragon and marry her. And in spite of his knowledge that she is now an old woman and no longer sensually attractive to him, he decides to venture out and look for the dragon.

⁵ Brigitte Prutti analyzes the role of the paintings in her thorough "Das Bild des Weiblichen und die Phantasie des Künstlers: Das Begehren des Prinzen in *Emilia Galotti*," *Zeitschrift für Deutsche Philologie* 110 (1991), 481–505.

⁶ In: *The Adapted Mind. Evolutionary Psychology and the Generation of Culture*, ed. Jerome H. Barkow, Leda Cosmides, John Tooby (New York: Oxford, 1992), 289–326, here 289–90.

⁷ Brigitte Prutti rightly refers to "die erotischen Wunschträume des voyeuristischen Bildbetrachters" (as note 5, 503).

⁸ Neill Flax takes the scene in which Odoardo stabs his daughter to be a *tableau vivant* that the audience would have recognized from the many pictorial

versions of the classical Virginia legend. He says that the *tableau vivant* is a moral counterpart to the Emilia portrait that aroused the Prince into action. Flax shows that Lessing and the Enlightenment in general hold that "until seeing is liberated from the tyranny of the senses, there will be no freedom for human beings." Neill Flax, "From Portrait to *tableau vivant*: The Pictures of *Emilia Galotti*," *Eighteen-Century Studies* 19 (1985), 39–55, the quotations are from p. 53 in the text and from p. 54 in the note. Brigitte Prutti, on the other hand, sees in Emilia's death the paradoxical fulfillment of the Prince's erotic desires as he expressed them when looking at the portrait: no one will now be able to rob him of his fantastic wishes (as note 5, 505).

[9] [This picture is bewitchingly beautiful,
Such as no eye has ever seen!
I feel how this divine image
Fills my heart with new stirring.
To be sure, I can't name this something,
But I feel it burn here like fire.
Could *this* sensation be love?
Yes, yes, it is pure love. —
O if only I could find her!
O if only she were to stand before me!
I would — would — warm and pure –
What would I? — I would, full of rapture,
Press her to this ardent breast;
then she would eternally be mine.]

Text according to the first edition, Vienna 1791, as reprinted in *Deutsche Literatur. Reihe Barock.* Vol. 1, *Die Maschinenkomödie*, ed. Otto Rommel (Leipzig: Reclam, 1935), 269–70.

[10] David Freedberg, *The Power of Images. Studies in History and Theory of Response* (Chicago and London: U of Chicago P, 1989), 338.

[11] In a similar vein Petra Fischer concludes: "Nicht zuletzt aus ihren Handlungen heraus resultiert Paminas und Taminos Prüfungsweg, der die Bedingung ihrer Vervollkommnung der Vorstellungskraft und somit ihrer endgültigen Vereinigung darstellt." [Ultimately it is primarily on the basis of their actions that Pamina's and Tamino's series of tests comes about which constitute the condition of their achieving perfection of their power of representation and thus of their final union]. "Die Rehabilitierung der Sinnlichkeit. Philosophische Implikationen der Figurenkonstellation der 'Zauberflöte,'" *Archiv für Musikwissenschaft* 50 [1993], 1–25, here 24.

2: Possession of a Woman by Design

Goethe: *Die Leiden des jungen Werthers*

The most extreme case of an artist appropriating to himself a woman by making her into a work of art I found in Edgar Allan Poe's story of 1842, "The Oval Portrait," also entitled "Life in Death." Here the artist paints his beautiful young wife and, being completely absorbed in his task, finally reaches the point when he exclaims "This is indeed *Life* itself!" Then "he turned suddenly to regard his beloved: — She was dead!" In German literature I have not found an equivalent situation in which the man is so much taken with his own art that he uses the woman only as an object. However, there is some resemblance between the artist's goal in Poe's story and what the Prince in Lessing's *Emilia Galotti* ultimately obtains, that is, her painting while she herself has been killed. At least this is Brigitte Prutti's theory to which I referred in the previous chapter when discussing Lessing's drama.

Each text I will review here has to do with the portrait of a woman that is appropriated by a man who is seen as the rival to the one she is engaged or married to. In some instances the possessor of the portrait is also the artist who painted or sketched or cut it out (there are two silhouettes). There is, then, in every case a triangle with the portrait functioning not only as a substitute for the woman herself but normally also causing increased tension among the three characters involved.

It is common knowledge that much of what Goethe used in *Die Leiden des jungen Werthers* [1774; 1789; The Sorrows of Young Werther] has its correspondence in his own life. Thus, the temptation is great to refer aspects of the fictional realm to those of Goethe's letters and other pieces of biographical evidence and vice versa. This interrelationship is especially fascinating in the case not only of *Werther* but also of Lenz's *Der Waldbruder* [The Hermit], a novel I will take up later in this chapter. Both authors made a fetish of the portrait of their beloved women. However, investigating the elusive area of biographical data and their emergence in those two works of fiction and even the possibility that these fictive creations in turn had a bearing on their author's lives, would lead us too far from the goal of this study, that is, from an analysis of men viewing women as art objects.

Werther possesses, among other talents, the ability to draw. While he is not a truly committed artist, he is, at least according to his own statement, a credible artist, who can, for instance, draw scenes of children against the background of a plow. He writes his second letter — addressed like the first to his friend Wilhelm — in the midst of a natural setting. In the letter, after echoing a remark by Conti, the painter in Lessing's *Emilia Galotti*, the tragedy that Werther seems to have been reading just before committing suicide, he claims that he is so saturated with the impressions of his surroundings that he has never been a greater artist than at this point — even though he is now unable to draw anything whatsoever. Naturally, he would have liked to paint Lotte's portrait and indeed makes three attempts at it but feels that he made an utter fool of himself every time ("prostituirt"; letter of July 24). He has to be satisfied with a silhouette. I see in this change from a full, three-dimensional portrait to a two-dimensional outline an indication of Werther's inability to grasp all of Lotte's personality. Such an inability to penetrate the world around him is especially noticeable in the case of the mother of the children Werther sketched. He envisions her spending her time in the narrow circle of a happy existence that will last year in year out when in reality one of her children was soon to die. In addition, her husband, who has to go to Switzerland to claim an inheritance due him, returns not only empty-handed but also a sick man.

In any case, Lotte's silhouette serves Werther as a substitute for Lotte herself: he greets it when returning to his room, says good-bye to it when leaving, and kisses it again and again. Shakespeare offers an excellent illustration of the situation when he has Proteus say to Silvia in *The Two Gentlemen of Verona*:

> Madam: if your heart be so obdurate,
> Vouchsafe me yet your picture for my love,
> The picture that is hanging in your chamber;
> For since the substance of your perfect self
> Is else devoted, I am but a shadow;
> And to your shadow will I make true love. (IV, 2, 116–122)

Werther had planned to take Lotte's silhouette down from the wall on the day of Lotte's and Albert's wedding and bury "her" among other papers (letter of February 20). The early editions have here "sie" (she) which can only refer to Lotte herself, not to the silhouette.[1] His thinly veiled violent nature with its occasional outbursts in a variety of threats manifests itself here in his attempt to "bury" Lotte once and for all on the day of her wedding to Albert.[2] In later editions the "sie" is changed to "ihn" (it) which refers to the silhouette and thus, while still ultimately pointing to Lotte herself since her silhouette is an equivalent to her as a person, tones down the directness of the wish as it is expressed in the original version.

Lotte and Albert had kept Werther in the dark about the exact date of their wedding and had informed him only after the fact. He decides to keep the silhouette on the wall and tries to comfort himself with the thought that he will remain dear to them and that he will and must continue to occupy a second place in Lotte's heart. Werther mentions the silhouette once more in his last letter to Lotte, a letter she will not receive until after his death. In that long letter, towards the end, he bequeaths the silhouette back to Lotte, thus completing the circle: the duplicate is returned to its original.

It becomes clear from the above analysis of Lotte's silhouette in *Werther* that its significance transcends the meaning a normal art object has for most people. The silhouette is in Werther's eyes Lotte herself, at least he would like to believe such an equivalence. But as little as he gets to be her lover and husband, just as little is the silhouette Lotte herself. Werther's world is thus an inauthentic one: he who strives for absolutes, for painting her three-dimensional portrait, has to be satisfied with the bare outline of her features, with her silhouette. We will hear echoes of such a relationship between the protagonist and his beloved in the next three texts.

Lenz: *Der Waldbruder*

Jakob Michael Reinhold Lenz's *Der Waldbruder* [The Hermit], "ein Pendant zum Werther" (a counterpart to Werther), as the subtitle states in the first edition (1797), goes back to 1776 and is considered a fragment. While Goethe's *Werther* consists in part of nonepistolary text, Lenz's novel is all letters that are written and addressed to a number of different persons. There is, then, no editor who takes over at any time.

The origin and destination of the portrait of the adored countess Stella is a very complicated one. Herz, the protagonist, now impoverished and living at the edge of society (thus the "Waldbruder"), is fully aware of the fact that he is unable, at least in his present condition, to have any chance with the wonderful Stella. He had read her letters at the house of a widow where he subsequently rented a room. Stella, who is engaged to Major Plettenberg, is told about how much the unbalanced Herz adores her and, out of pity, talks to him at the widow's house. She also consents to have her portrait painted there by an artist whom Herz believes he has engaged. Herz thus has ample time to study every nuance of Stella's appearance while she is sitting for the artist and enjoys every moment of these sessions. He is ignorant of the fact that Stella is engaged to Plettenberg, who, in turn, has asked Herz to accompany him to America where Plettenberg intends to prove his valor fighting the revolutionaries so as to impress, once he has been promoted to the rank of general or lieutenant general, Stella's father before asking for her hand. Herz believes that he is to be given the original of Stella's portrait, with a copy going to his good friend Rothe. Actually, it was Rothe who had arranged Stella's sessions with the artist; in addition, Herz was not to have either the original or the copy of the painting. When he is faced with the imminent departure to America and the prospect of going without her ("ohne sie"), that is, without Stella's portrait, his talisman, he is enraged and writes a threatening letter to Rothe who in turn pleads successfully with Plettenberg to let Herz have the painting.

Herz is an emasculated romantic whose idealization of women works as a safeguard against ever having to have physical contact with a woman. To be sure, he succeeds in talking to Stella and in looking at her at length but it is not he who paints her — Werther, after all, had made his own silhouette of Lotte — but someone else. From now on the portrait takes the place of Stella herself. All his endeavors are directed toward obtaining the painting. There is no longer any attempt to approach Stella in person. He is ready to murder Rothe, at least those are his words, if Rothe does not give back the portrait. His entire life seems to depend on having Stella in the form of an art object near him. Both when Stella is being painted and then after she has been duplicated on canvas, she poses no threat to Herz; rather, he can study her in peace and let his imagination wander freely.

In the introduction to this chapter I mentioned that men become jealous when they learn that the portrait of the beloved is in the hands of another man. The complicated maneuver that led to Stella's being painted in the presence of Herz had been carried out without Plettenberg's, her fiancé's, knowledge. Here is the explanation for the secrecy:

> Sie hat sich wirklich für Herzen malen lassen, wobei die Witwe Hohl immer die Hand mit im Spiel gehabt, weil Plettenberg dies nicht erfahren sollte. Sie wissen, die Delikatesse eines Liebhabers kann durch nichts so sehr beleidigt werden, als auch nur das Bild von seiner Angebeteten in fremden Händen zu wissen.[3]

When Rothe finally explains the situation to Plettenberg and tells him of Herz's precarious emotional state of mind and how much that state of mind is connected with the possession of the portrait, he agrees to let Herz have it. His consent comes most reluctantly, as is shown by his letter to Rothe, the last letter in the fragmentary novel:

> In der Tat, mein lieber Rothe, habe ich Ursache von diesem Ihrem Verfahren gegen mich ein wenig beleidigt zu sein, besonders aber von der Gewissenhaftigkeit, mit der Sie alles das von mir verschwiegen gehalten. Ich hatte das Herz nicht, dieses seinsollende Porträt meiner Braut Herzen zu entziehen, weil ich fürchtete seine Gemütskrankheit dadurch in Wut zu verwandeln, aber es kränkt mich doch daß ein Bild von ihr in fremden und noch dazu in so unzuverlässigen Händen bleiben soll.[4]

Clearly, Plettenberg acknowledges the misgivings of the man who is engaged to a woman to see her portrait, her duplicate, in another man's possession. Again, art is here substituted for life and there is the implied belief that the artistic duplicate contains some aspect of the live original.

As a fragment *Der Waldbruder* leaves the ultimate fate of the main character undecided. However, as in its model, as in *Werther*, it is clear that in the long run the portrait will not be a legitimate substitute for the beloved. To be sure, the visual representation can easily be subjected to unimpeded viewing and even kisses but it is ultimately an object that cannot change and is thus at best a memory. Goethe could work out his emotional crisis by writing *Werther*;

Lenz, in spite of fascinating insights into the unstable character of his protagonist Herz, that is, into his own character, could not come to terms with himself and society. He predicted his own breakdown in the figure of Herz who looks for the ideal woman and, after finding her, has to be content with her portrait.

Plenzdorf: *Die neuen Leiden des jungen W.*

The extraordinary seminal power of Goethe's *Werther* is shown by the many parodies and recastings that the novel has engendered. Of special importance is the delightful reworking of Goethe's work to the German Democratic Republic in the form of Ulrich Plenzdorf's 1973 novel *Die neuen Leiden des jungen W.* [The New Sorrows of the Young W.]. At the beginning of the novel Edgar, an apprentice in a factory in boring Mittenberg, decides to go to Berlin where there is more action, especially as far as the rock music scene is concerned. He settles into an abandoned cabin that stands next to a kindergarten. Charlie, as Edgar calls her, is one of the teachers there and plays the role of Werther's Lotte. Edgar's painting ability is even less than that of Werther, but like his model he is able to make a silhouette of Charlie which he keeps even though she wants it. He claims that it is as yet not finished, that it doesn't have any life in it. Of course it does not since a silhouette cannot do justice to Charlie's beautiful features, including her black eyes, that is, eyes of the same color as those of Werther's Lotte. He calls them "Scheinwerfer" (headlights) and is beside himself whenever she looks at him. Charlie is upset when Edgar insists on keeping the silhouette. She correctly senses that this is an indication of his love for her which she does not want to reciprocate. She is fond of Edgar, just as Lotte is fond of Werther, but Charlie wants the silhouette for Dieter, her fiancé who is in the army. When Dieter, a bit later, is discharged and both he and Charlie visit Edgar in the cabin, they look at the "abstract" paintings on the walls. These paintings amount to nothing more than doodlings with color. Dieter, patterned on Albert in *Werther*, mentions the need for rules and proportion in which Edgar is of course not in the least interested. Then Dieter discovers Charlie's silhouette which Edgar must have placed in such a way that he could look at it easily. Charlie immediately tells Dieter that the silhouette was meant for him and that Edgar had kept it so as to finish it but he had not done anything with it since her sitting for him. Dieter does not sense that Edgar thus has a claim on Charlie, that he has kept the silhouette as a substitute for the real person. All Dieter has to say to Charlie is that he now has the actual Charlie and thus dismisses the thought that her silhouette has any meaning besides a piece of paper. Like Albert, Dieter is preoccupied with his career and is just as much a matter-of-fact person. Thus, Dieter does not seem to be capable of jealousy. Still, Edgar has to be satisfied with one ecstatic moment of closeness to the real Charlie when the two kiss during a wild boat ride. Soon afterwards Edgar is killed when the high-powered paint spray gun which he was developing blows up.

We have in *Die neuen Leiden des jungen W.* an interesting version of the *Werther* triangle, with the silhouette playing a similar role in both novels. While in Goethe's story Werther sends the silhouette to Lotte before committing suicide and thus tries to increase her feelings of sorrow and guilt for having lost him, Charlie's silhouette is plowed under with the rest of Edgar's belongings after his death when a bulldozer levels the area for new construction. Edgar is a more sensible character than Werther and never mentions anything like those many kisses and good-byes Werther directed to Lotte's portrait. Still, having Charlie's silhouette in his possession was something that meant a lot to him, that is, the duplicate of his beloved Charlie.

Goethe: *Der Triumph der Empfindsamkeit*

Werther's kissing Lotte's silhouette and Herz's finding in the beloved woman's portrait a complete substitute for the real person are followed by Goethe's *Der Triumph der Empfindsamkeit* [first produced in 1778, first printed in 1786; The Triumph of Sentimentality], a satirical comedy on sentimentality. That Goethe has both his own novel and Lenz's *Waldbruder* in mind when writing *Der Triumph der Empfindsamkeit* can be seen by the fact that *Werther* is one of the novels that have affected a character of the satire, the Prince, with a severe attack of sentimentality and that the Prince's favored word is "Herz," both a leitmotiv in *Werther* and the name of Lenz's "Waldbruder."[5] A typical sentence, coming at the end of *Der Triumph der Empfindsamkeit*, is the Prince's address to his beloved, actually a stuffed doll: "Hier, hier ist meine Gottheit, die ganz mein

Herz nach ihrem Herzen zieht!" ["Here, here is my idol that pulls my heart fully to her heart!"].

In Goethe's satire, the Prince has fallen in love with Mandandane, the wife of the jovial king Andrason. The Prince has helped Mandandane act out some melodramas, and she believes that he is in love with her refined spirituality, that he loves her company for the conversations they have on the tender feelings of their hearts. In reality, unbeknownst to her, he has fallen in love with her duplicate, a stuffed doll that, like Madame Tussaud's wax figures, is an exact replica of the real Mandandane. Essential for the effect the doll has on the Prince is its inner core. It consists of a sack that contains chaff that covers a number of sentimental novels, among them the above-mentioned *Werther*. It is this core that has the magic effect on the Prince and lets him dissolve his erotic desire in cliché outpourings of sentimental verbiage directed at the stuffed doll. He has Mandandane's replica placed in an arbor and surrounded by the requisite landscape including artificial moonlight and all the other trappings that belong to the cult of sentimentality. In order to be able to pursue his favorite pastime even when away from his castle, he has an ingenious craftsman make a number of boxes and a variety of contraptions so that the arbor and everything else can be erected wherever the Prince's travels take him.

At the castle belonging to the sister of Mandandane's husband, Andrason, the Prince spends the first evening in the arbor, holding the doll's hand and reciting trashy, sentimental verses. With the help of the curiosity of the women in attendance at the court, Andrason finds out the Prince's secret. Mandandane, who is alienated from her husband since he doesn't share her and the Prince's cult of sentimentality, comes to her sister-in-law's castle and is told about the Prince's aberration. She cannot believe that he could be so childish, but agrees to test him by dressing in exactly the same clothes her duplicate is wearing and sitting in the same position in the arbor. In that moment the Prince returns. He is at odds with the message of an enigmatic oracle he has just received according to which he should return to the rightful owner that which he had foolishly stolen and thus come into possession of that which he had borrowed with so much anxiety. The Prince correctly interprets the first part of the saying as meaning that he should give up Mandandane, something he is most loath to do since the most enjoyable moments he spends are with her, that is, with her dummy. When faced with the real Mandandane as her own duplicate, the Prince, however, is no longer at odds with the first part of the message of the oracle. He is now willing to give her up. As he says, it seems to him that a strange woman has taken the place of his beloved. Thus, a reconciliation is possible between the repentant Mandandane and her admirable, wise husband. The Prince, on the other hand, is besides himself with joy when he is shown the stuffed doll with its magic core, the sentimental novels that make the person turn from reality to silly game playing with duplicates of life and nature, with narcissistic projections, and ultimately with death. He thus comes again into possession of things he had borrowed as the second part of the oracle had predicted. As soon as the Prince sees the stuffed duplicate of Mandandane, he can indulge again in his amorous longings and start reciting the same trashy and sentimental verses we had heard before: the mechanism of sentimental indulgence can be wound up again and is safe from surprises since other men have been eliminated.

I had mentioned in discussing Lenz's *Waldbruder* that Herz feels safer with the inanimate object, the adored woman's portrait, than with the woman herself. The portrait thus takes over as the object desired and worried about. In *Der Triumph der Empfindsamkeit* Goethe clearly takes this deviation from a normal relationship between the sexes to its extreme and has the man react amorously to the adored woman only when that woman appears in the form of a dummy. Obviously, we have here a satire on an incident in Lenz's own life about which Goethe and the Weimar society were well aware and on the strange behavior of Herz, the protagonist of Lenz's *Der Waldbruder*. In the case of Herz we assume that he will keep the portrait of the beloved. And nobody is going to interfere with the Prince's tête-à-tête with Mandandane's dummy that is placed in the middle of an artificial landscape. Art and artifice have been substituted for reality as the focus of the desire of the emasculated men in the novel by Lenz and in the satire by Goethe. If Goethe needed to distance himself from his own sentimentality — beyond the masterful way that was accomplished in *Werther* — *Der Triumph der Empfindsamkeit* certainly put any such tendency behind him. As an author he will not create any more characters who fall in love with the portraits of the beloved woman or even with their dummies.[6]

Dorothea Schlegel: *Florentin*

While one can possess an art object, one cannot "possess" another human being. To be sure, men have tried to consider women their property, but such ownership is of course never complete. As we have observed in the previous examples, the male desire to "possess" the beloved woman can be diverted to a possession of the beloved's duplicate, in the form of a painting or a dummy. That having the duplicate implies a certain control over the real person is an idea that is brought out clearly in the next two novels.

Toward the end of Dorothea Schlegel's *Florentin* (1801) there is a scene that shows a most violent reaction of a man — he is Walter, a captain — who is vainly trying to obtain from the artist the sketch he had just made. The sketch is of Walter's fiancée Betty. The artist is Florentin, the protagonist of Schlegel's novel, who is not only a competent painter but also a poet and accomplished musician. He is, as Goethe observed after reading a good part of the novel, an extraordinary human being, just the sort of hero any student would like to be (letter to Schiller, March 18, 1801). Florentin is young, unattached, apparently, at least at the time the novel takes place, without financial worries, and in search of his parents as well as of his destiny. Thus, he is greatly admired by women and also by men, with the exception of Walter, Betty's fiancé. She is the attractive, lively and trusted companion and confidante of the wealthy Clementina who is the spiritual center of a group of people and also the supporter of a large number of needy families.

Florentin, on his way to visit with Clementina, first stops at an inn and there runs into Walter. Both of them develop an immediate and extreme dislike for each other. Walter tries unsuccessfully to make Florentin the butt of his jokes and thus to live up to his reputation among his comrades as a witty man of the world. Florentin, of course, knows how to turn the tables on Walter and feels very strongly that Betty, about whose engagement to Walter he has been informed, should under no circumstances marry him. Finally, Florentin cannot stand Walter's unpleasantries any longer and leaves the inn with Clementina's kind physician. They walk over to his garden where Betty tells them that her mistress is, as happens regularly, indisposed and therefore unable to greet Florentin about whose arrival she knows.

In the course of the conversation between Florentin, the physician, and Betty, the suggestion is made that Florentin cut Betty's silhouette. He decides rather to draw her:

> Sie stellte sich in einer leichten angenehmen Stellung vor ihn hin. Mit wenigen Strichen war das Figürchen entworfen, im schwebenden Tanz mit beiden Händen ein Tamburin in die Höhe haltend, Gesicht und Haltung, obgleich nur in flüchtigen Umrissen, zum Sprechen ähnlich. Florentin war vergnügt mit dem Entwurf, er hatte seiner Hand nicht mehr diese Sicherheit zugetraut.[7]

Florentin has thus expressed in his sketch Betty's true personality, the way she would like to be even with or especially with Walter. It is Walter, though, who squelches the lively and fun-loving side of his fiancée. At that moment Walter joins them and the following exchange of words among the four occurs:

> "Lassen Sie doch sehen," fuhr Walter fort, indem er näher zum Tisch trat, wo die Zeitung lag; "Sie haben hier eine Akademie wie ich sehe; die Künste werden doch immer mehr getrieben in der Welt!" — Florentin kam ihm zuvor, als jener das Blatt in die Hand nehmen wollte. Er verdeckte es schnell mit einem anderen Blatt. "Entschuldigen Sie," sagte er kurz und trocken, "es ist nicht fertig." — "Mir können Sie es immer halb fertig zeigen, ich bin gar kein Kenner." — "Um desto weniger Herr Rittmeister!" — "Es ist Fräulein Betty ihr Porträt, das habe ich gesehen." — "Allerdings ist es das." — "Nun so muß ich Ihnen dann sagen: ich habe ein Recht dazu es zu fordern." — "Das mag sein, aber ich habe kein Recht, es Ihnen zu geben, es gehört dem Fräulein." — "Sie werden also entscheiden Fräulein," rief er aufgebracht. — "In der Tat lieber Walter ... es war ein Scherz ... ich bat darum." — "Nun so wird man es doch wenigstens erkaufen können; was ist ihr Preis?" fragte er, seine Börse hervorziehend. — Florentin antwortete nicht, und legte das Blatt mit Gelassenheit in sein Taschenbuch. — "Es ist nicht für Bezahlung gemacht, lieber Walter," sagte Betty wieder. — "Es muß doch auf irgendeine Weise wieder in Ihre Hände kommen, denn weder ich, noch Sie selbst werden zugeben, daß Ihr Bild in der Welt mit auf Abenteuer zieht." — "Herr Rittmeister!" sagte hier der Doktor mit fester Stimme, "Sie scheinen zu vergessen, daß Sie hier in meinem Hause sind!" — "Ich werde diesem ehrwürdigen Hause nicht länger beschwerlich fallen." — Hohnlachend, und aufgedunsen von wildem Zorn fuhr er zur Tür hinaus. — "O Ihr wißt nicht, was Ihr mir tut!" rief Betty voller Angst, und ging ihm nach.[8]

It is interesting to note that Florentin uses the same excuse for not parting with the sketch he made as Edgar in Ulrich Plenzdorf's *Die neuen Leiden des jungen W.* when Charlie asks him for the silhouette he made of her. Both Florentin and Edgar claim that their portraits are as yet not finished and in both cases the claim is made in order to keep the sketch or the silhouette. I have quoted the passage from *Florentin* in full because we have here an excellent example of how an author brings out the meaning the portrait of a woman can have for a man who in his mind believes that he has a hold on her. Walter needs to maintain his control of Betty whom he wants to marry, not out of love but for the money he expects her to have from the wealthy Clementina. The monetary aspect comes out clearly in his offer to pay Florentin for the sketch that has become the equivalent of the person portrayed. Just as the Prince in *Emilia Galotti* is hoping to buy Emilia herself when he buys the portrait from Conti, Walter is trying to buy Betty. In addition, with her portrait in someone else's possession, he fears that he will lose some of his hold on her.

The novel does not tell us about what ultimately happens to Betty and Walter. All we learn in the last few pages following the incident with the sketch is that there is a duel between Walter and Florentin in which Walter resorts to foul play while Florentin manages to take the sword away from Walter which he then breaks to pieces and throws at Walter's feet. Thus, the male who puts down women is put down himself and is left without his masculine attribute. For my purpose it is important to observe how the portrait of a woman is again the equivalent of the woman herself and how the egocentric attitude and possessive male convention is undermined in *Florentin*, a novel written by a woman. Betty's personality is recognized by the positive male character who draws her in a dancing motion and thus reveals her desire to enjoy life in her own way.

After having disarmed Walter, Florentin magnanimously lets him go and then leaves town: "Florentin war nirgends zu finden" [Florentin was not to be found anywhere] is the last sentence of the fragmentary novel. Still, the incident with the sketch might very well have been the last straw in the already strained relationship between the charming, lively Betty and the arrogant Walter, one of the most despicable characters I have come across in the novels of the time. He easily tops in his wretchedness and his abusive treatment of Betty the "so genannten Herrn Schmidt" [the so-called Mr. Schmidt] whose face turns dark when Werther flirts a bit with his fiancée in Goethe's *Die Leiden des jungen Werthers* (letter of July 1). Walter, in all probability, is left in the end without Betty and definitely without her sketch.

Fanny Lewald: *Jenny*

Fanny Lewald's novel *Jenny* appeared in 1841. The protagonist, the daughter of wealthy and enlightened Jewish parents, grows up in a German town where Jews were tolerated but where they were, if possible, kept out of the best social circles. Also, they were not allowed to hold public office. While her brilliant brother Konrad embarks on a most successful career as a physician and refuses to convert to Christianity even though that means not being able to marry the girl he is deeply in love with (and she with him) as well as not becoming the director of the city hospital, Jenny converts in order to marry Gustav Reinhard.[9] Jenny is unusually beautiful, intelligent, talented, and somewhat spoiled. One of her many admirers is Erlau, a painter and also her art teacher. In contrast to Reinhard, Erlau is the fun-loving artistic type who loves social gatherings. At one point he organizes a tableau vivant party at which Jenny is the main attraction. Appropriately enough, he casts her as the daughter in Eduard Bendemann's "Trauernde Juden" (Mourning Jews), as Recha in Lessing's *Nathan der Weise* (Nathan the Wise), and as Rebecca in Sir Walter Scott's *Ivanhoe*. At one point Erlau requests to paint Jenny dressed as Rebecca, a request she grants with the understanding that the portrait will be given to Reinhard.[10] A little bit later Jenny is painting the scene she sees from the balcony of her house. Erlau is standing next to her and uses the opportunity to declare his love for her. He takes out a small brooch which he opens. Inside is Jenny's portrait in the costume of Rebecca. She is taken aback and is unsure of what to say. He uses her silence to tell her that all he wants is to be sure that she will always strive for the beautiful in her life and thus preserve her pure image in his memory. She gladly promises him that she will try to live up to his expectations. Erlau, now that he has made his confession, can leave for Italy to further his career. When he has left, Jenny reflects on the difference between Erlau and Reinhard and realizes that Erlau's going away also means the end of the playful part of her life. The author has her feel so uncertain about the incident that just happened that she has Jenny keep her knowledge of Erlau's departure a secret, even to Reinhard, a resolve that will make her lie later on. Jenny has rather contradictory feelings about the portrait Erlau has painted and kept. She doesn't begrudge him his painting it but chides herself for having let him keep it. It was the portrait of her that Erlau had promised to give to Reinhard but had made instead all kinds of excuses for not having finished it. She could not help but be flattered by his silent love for her. The scene she had just painted and had wanted to give to her fiancé she now throws into the air and sees it float to the nearby river. She did not want Reinhard to find pleasure in something that Erlau had looked at with tears in his eyes.

Knowing Jenny's and Reinhard's characters, it comes as no surprise to the reader after this episode that the two do not get married. As a matter of fact, a rival in Jenny's love of Reinhard has witnessed the scene in which Erlau said good-bye to Jenny and uses the information to drive a wedge between her and Reinhard.

With the portrait of Jenny, Lewald brings out, on the one hand, Jenny's character and then also the attraction she feels for a man like Erlau. He represents a part of her that enjoys life, its artistic and fun-loving aspects. Thus, she really does not mind knowing that he possesses her portrait, that he will remember her as the witty, talented, beautiful, and universally adored young woman. We had indications already in *Die Leiden des jungen Werthers* that the talented protagonist represents that part of Lotte's life that tends toward enjoyment in society. She knows that once married to Albert that type of life will be squashed. Similarly, Florentin in Dorothea Schlegel's novel sketches Betty in a dancing position, an aspect of her character that Walter, her fiancé, finds utterly repugnant. Betty does not object to Florentin's sketching her portrait in that way nor to his keeping it. Nor does Jenny when Erlau has painted her as Rebecca. The artists in each case capture aspects of the women they portray that their fiancés are unable or unwilling to respond to.

Erlau's casting of Jenny in the various tableaux vivants is of course used by the author to foreshadow her fate. As the daughter in Eduard Bendemann's "Trauernde Juden," at the time a popular painting, she reflects the general homelessness of Jews in the Diaspora. As Recha, Jenny mirrors Nathan's enlightened child in Lessing's play. Recha does not get to marry the beloved Templar since it turns out that they are brother and sister. And just as little does Rebecca in Sir Walter Scott's novel of 1819 get to marry her beloved Ivanhoe whom she had nursed back to health and who had, in turn, rescued her from being burned at the stake as a sorceress. Through Erlau's selection of roles for Jenny, Lewald thus brings out on the one hand Jenny's enlightened outlook and on the other her being, because of her religion, an outsider in the society in which she lives and in which she cannot find permanent happiness in spite of being admired by ever so many men. Her memory, though, will live on in the hearts of many, including Erlau who has her portrait as an ideal memento. In Theodor Storm's *Immensee*, a novella I will analyze in chapter VII, the portrait of the beloved woman is such a memento for the protagonist and will trigger the reminiscences that make up the story.

Thomas Mann: *Felix Krull*

Erlau, the painter in Fanny Lewald's *Jenny*, belongs to the tradition of the Romantic artist who admires female beauty for its own sake. At least that is what he professes to do when he, after declaring his love for Jenny, leaves her and goes to Italy. He finds a substitute for the possession of the living woman in taking along her portrait that will be the focus of his memories of Jenny. In Thomas Mann's *Die Bekenntnisse des Hochstaplers Felix Krull* [1954; The Confessions of the Confidence Man Felix Krull] the protagonist and narrator does not believe in anything but the enhancement of his own person in the eyes of the reader. Nothing is authentic in his life; at the end of the novel he impersonates and substitutes for Louis de Venosta, a bon vivant, who wants to stay in Paris with his mistress, Zaza, rather than go on a trip his wealthy parents have mapped out for him to break their son's liaison. Louis de Venosta lets his double, that is, Felix, take along on the trip to Lisbon, the first station on the planned tour, sketches of the naked Zaza.

Once in Lisbon, Felix gets involved in the same triangular situation that Goethe's Werther and his successors exemplified, that is, pursuing a woman who is already engaged. The protagonist, whether Werther, Herz, Florentin or Felix, intrudes on a couple where the man is the serious type and represents the socially accepted norm while the protagonist is an outsider who has leanings towards the artistic and the adventurous. In the case of Felix there is the beautiful Suzanna or Zouzou as she is called, daughter of Senhora Kuckuck. Zouzou is engaged to Miguel Hurtado, a taxidermist and animal sculptor who works for Professor Kuckuck, the director of the Lisbon museum of natural history.

After first meeting Zouzou, Felix had added to Louis de Venosta's sketches of the naked Zaza strains of hair on her temples so as to make the sketches look somewhat more like Zouzou. Since the originals did not portray Zaza in an accurate manner — Louis de Venosta had no talent as a painter — the sketches could easily be mistaken for those of Zouzou. Felix uses the existence of the drawing in a most ingenious way to arouse Zouzou's erotic interest in him. There are many obstacles to their meeting in privacy. In addition to the fact that Portuguese society does not allow unmarried couples to meet by themselves, Zouzou rejects all talk and behavior that tends toward the erotic as something indecent and finds even the thought of touching a man's body utterly unappetizing. Felix, on the other hand, is his most eloquent self when praising the raptures of the senses and the bliss of becoming one as lovers. He had told Zouzou of the existence of the drawings, a ploy that brings the long awaited get-together. Zouzou is of course enraged when first learning of their existence, which she thinks are the product of his sexual fantasies. She demands that they be given to her since she has, as the one being portrayed, a right to them. Whenever the two meet, she brings up the topic and chides him for not carrying out her request. Cunningly, he delays turning the sketches over to her since they constitute a link between them, something that only they know about. Also, there is uncertainty on his part as to how she would take to these rather daring sketches.

It is fascinating to observe that both Zouzou and Felix see in his having possession of the sketches an equivalent or near equivalent of his having a certain control over her. Zouzou feels that a part of her is in Felix's hands as a part of Martha is in the hands of her first husband who bought her portrait in Mary McCarthy's *A Charmed Life*. I want to quote from a statement the painter in Mary McCarthy's novel makes. He mentions that Martha has a stake in the painting since she sat for him and then adds:

In Mexico, they'll break your camera if you try to take a picture of their dances. They believe you're stealing their soul. And there's a lot of that in all of us, let me tell you.[11]

When Zouzou learns that her naked figure — actually it is of course Zaza's naked figure — is in Felix's hands, she becomes, as mentioned above, furious. Then, however, softened by Felix's appeal to the erotic and his eloquent praise of universal love and, specifically, of her beauty, she is more and more impressed by his courtship and is finally taken in by his attractive personality. Now *she* uses the sketches and tells him where and when to come to a clandestine meeting so that he can hand over the tell-tale studies. Her reaction to seeing what she thinks is her own naked figure is as to be expected: first she blushes, then she tears up the various sheets and starts hitting him with her fists while, at the same time, passionately embracing him and responding eagerly to his kisses. The novel, at least the part Mann finished, ends with Senhora Kuckuck's breaking up the scene and claiming Felix for herself.

Thomas Mann's use of the implications that go with the possession of the beloved's portrait is nothing if not masterful. In the previous examples the protagonist has always been a sincere admirer of the woman involved, the woman who was already engaged to the less attractive but socially more acceptable man. Felix is never sincere. He is not the artist who had made the sketches. He is not truly in love with Zouzou; rather, he wants to show the reader that he is capable of seducing a woman as attractive as Zouzou. While his predecessors had honestly admired the woman involved, even had put her on a pedestal as in the case of Werther, Herz, and Erlau, Felix wants to show off his power of persuasion and his supposedly irresistible appeal to women. In the process he uses designs made by Louis de Venosta, designs that he claims are his own and of Zouzou when in reality they are of Zaza, to seduce Zouzou. Even in connection with the women's portraits, Felix Krull reveals himself to be what he really is, a confidence man. It is in this respect that we admire him, at least secretly, for his exploits and his exciting adventures. As in the case of all picaros, Felix is in the eyes of the reader both a figure of envy and a figure of disapproval. In contrast to the Spanish picaresque models where the narrators/protagonists look back on their past and realize that that past was sinful, Felix shows no such remorse. The critical attitude in his case must come from the reader. It is easy to see how he embellishes such criminal actions as the stealing of candy when he was a boy, or, later on, as his becoming a pimp in Frankfurt. The use of Louis de Venosta's sketches is less easily seen as something immoral. Still, Felix here again shows his ability to take on a new persona, that of the wealthy nobleman in love, and to use his linguistic skills to seduce a woman not because he really loves her and wants to establish a permanent relationship with her, but so as to impress the reader and possibly himself that he is capable of these things, that he is also a Don Juan.

In his seduction of Zouzou, Felix cleverly uses the sketches of the naked Zaza to bring about the desired rendezvous with Zouzou. After destroying what she thinks are the products of his imagination, which she finds offensive on the one hand but also flattering and secretly exciting, she offers herself to him. Felix has used his psychological insights and the drawings to gain the woman he wanted to add to the list of his conquests.

The seven works taken up in this chapter show a variety of patterns that develop in connection with the origin of a woman's portrait or her doll-like duplicate and the consequences. For one, there is the man who is her fiancé or her husband. Depending on his sensitivity and possessiveness, he reacts with the apparent indifference (Albert in *Werther*, Dieter in *Die neuen Leiden*) or annoyance (Plettenberg in *Der Waldbruder*) or outrage (Walter in *Florentin*). The woman involved, on the other hand, is normally impressed by the attention the artist or the person buying her portrait has bestowed on her. Lotte, one might speculate, senses that Werther's understanding of her is ultimately rather superficial when he cannot come up with more than a silhouette. Mandandane in *Der Triumph der Empfindsamkeit* is utterly taken aback when she finds out that the Prince, with whom she shares the cult of sentimentality, is really infatuated with a dummy to which he can direct his amorous addresses. Betty in *Florentin* as well as Jenny in Lewald's novel are appreciative of the artist who brought out in their portraits aspects of their personality that their straight-laced fiancés did not condone. Zouzou in *Felix Krull* is, as we have just seen, the one who discovers her own sensuality when seeing the sketches of what she believes is her naked body. The designing Felix, in contrast to many of his predecessors who were often content or at least were resigned to viewing the adored woman as an art object, uses sketches that he supposedly drew of the naked Zouzou to make her yield to him.

Notes

[1] The original text has: "und hatte mir vorgenommen, feyerlichst an demselben [Tag] Lottens Schattenriß von der Wand zu nehmen und sie unter andere Papiere zu begraben" [and had planned to take down from the wall in a solemn act Lotte's silhouette and on that day to bury her under other papers.]
   As is well known, the textual history of *Die Leiden des jungen Werther* is a very complicated one. The Weimar edition has "ihn" in the text and refers to the various editions that have "sie."

[2] On Werther's potential for violence see Thomas P. Saine, "Passion and Aggression: The Meaning of Werther's Last Letter," *Orbis Litterarum* 35 (1980), 327–56, specifically 333–4 and 338–9.

[3] [She actually let herself be painted for Herz, an undertaking in which the widow Hohl was constantly involved because Plettenberg was not supposed to know about this. You are aware that a lover's sensitivity cannot be offended by anything as much as knowing that the portrait of his adored is in the hands of another person.]
   Jakob Michael Reinhold Lenz, *Werke und Brief in drei Bänden*, ed. Sigrid Damm (Munich: Hanser, 1987), vol II, 406.

[4] [As a fact, my dear Rothe, I do have cause to be a bit offended by your procedure toward me, especially by the care you took to keep all this secret from me. I didn't have the heart to take away from Herz the portrait of my fiancée, a portrait that he claims belongs to him, because I was afraid to change his melancholy by this action into rage; but I still am vexed by the fact that her portrait is to remain in another person's hands, hands that are moreover so unreliable.] Ibid., 412.

[5] One could argue that *Der Waldbruder* was not published until 1797 and that the "Herz" allusion could not have been known to Goethe nor to the Weimar society in 1778 when *Der Triumph der Empfindsamkeit* was first produced. However, Goethe had obtained the manuscript at an earlier time, before 1778. It could also well be that others at the court were familiar with the manuscript.

[6] The latest analysis of Goethe's satire is by Hellmut Ammerlahn, "Vom Püppchen zum Liebchen, vom Schatten zur erkennenden Frau. Ironische und therapeutische Selbstinszenierungen der dichterischen Phantasie in Goethe's 'Anti-Werther-Dramen' *Lila* und *Triumph der Empfindsamkeit*," in: *Analogon Rationis. Festschrift für Gerwin Marsh zum 65. Geburtstag*, ed. Marianne Henn and Christoph Lorey. (Edmonton, Alberta: U of Alberta P, 1994), 111–28. Ammerlahn's focus is rather different from mine. There is no reference to "Herz" nor to Lenz. Also different as to focus is Astrid Lange-Kirchheim's

"Spiel im Spiel — Traum im Traum. Zum Zusammenhang von Goethe's *Triumph der Empfindsamkeit* und dem Monodrama *Proserpina*." While she mentions the Prince's narcissism, she stresses the way Goethe reacted to the death of his sister Cornelia when creating the figure of Proserpina. In: *Psychoanalytische und psychopathologische Literaturinterpretation*, ed. Bernd Urban und Winfried Kudszus (Darmstadt: Wissenschaftliche Buchgesellschaft, 1981), 125–51.

7 [She placed herself in front of him in a graceful, comfortable position. The little figure had been sketched with a few lines. She was suspended in a dancing position, holding up with both hands a tambourine, face and posture, even though only sketched in quick outline, her exact likeness. Florentin was happy with the sketch, he hadn't believed that his hand had this certainty any more.] Dorothea Schlegel, *Florentin. Ein Roman. Herausgegeben von Friedrich Schlegel*, vol. 1, ed. Paul Kluckohn. *Deutsche Literatur. Reihe Romantik*, vol. 7 (Leipzig: Reclam, 1933), 223.

8 ["Let me see," continued Walter while stepping closer to the table on which the sketch lay, "you have here an academy, as I see; the arts are flourishing in this world, after all!" Florentin anticipated Walter's move when he tried to take the sheet. Florentin quickly covered it with another sheet. "Excuse me," he said shortly and in a dry voice, "it isn't finished." — "You can just the same show it to me even if it is only half finished, I am not a connoisseur." — "Then it is even more out of the question, Captain!" — "It is Mademoiselle Betty's portrait, I saw that much." — "Indeed, it is." — "Then I have to tell you that I have a right to demand it." — "That may be, but I do not have the right to give it to you, it belongs to Mademoiselle." — "Then you will decide, Mademoiselle," he called being very agitated. — "Indeed, my dear Walter . . . it was a jest . . . I asked to have it done." — "Well, then one will at least be able to purchase it; what is the price?" he asked, pulling out his wallet. — Florentin didn't answer and calmly placed the sheet in his note book. — "It wasn't made to be sold, my dear Walter," said Betty. — "But it must get back into your hands in some way because neither I nor yourself will allow that your picture will go along on adventures all over the world." — "Captain!" the Doctor said with a firm voice, "you seem to forget that you are here in my house!" — "I shall no longer be a burden to this venerable house." — Laughing scornfully and puffed up with a wild rage, he rushed out of the door. — "Oh, you don't know what you are doing to me!" Betty cried full of fright and followed him.] Ibid., 223–4.

9 Strangely enough, while most of the other characters in the novel are called by their first name, Gustav is usually referred to by his last, that is, Reinhard. This oddity does not stand out very much since Reinhard is also a first name. Still, the author indicates in this way a certain distance between narrator and character and thus also creates distance between the character and the reader.

10 The text is not quite clear here. I interpret the phrase "Erlau besaß ihr Bild, das für Reinhard zu malen er immer unter neuen Vorwänden sich gewei-

gert hatte" [Erlau had in his possession her portrait that he had refused to paint for Reinhard, offering all kinds of pretexts] as referring to the portrait Erlau had painted of Jenny in the costume of Rebecca (Fanny Lewald, *Jenny. Historischer Roman* [Berlin: Der Morgen, 1967]), 175.

[11]   Mary McCarthy, *A Charmed Life* (New York: Harcourt, Brace and Co., 1954, 1955), 67.

3: Prophetic Vision

Goethe: *Wilhelm Meisters Lehrjahre*

The art with which Goethe integrated the "Bild vom kranken Königssohn" [Painting of the Sick Prince] into the narrative of *Wilhelm Meisters Lehrjahre* [1795–1796; Wilhelm Meister's Apprenticeship] is truly outstanding. Careful study reveals that Goethe avoids a long description of the painting when it is introduced. While it is first mentioned at the end of book one, the last detail about its content is only found at the very end of the novel, in book eight. We have here a perfect demonstration of how something that depicts a single moment in time is changed to a narrative sequence. Thus, Lessing's observation on the difference between painting and sculpture on the one hand and literature on the other finds its confirmation and application in Goethe's novel.

First of all, I will describe the scene depicted in the painting. The background can be found in the works of several authors, among them in the biography of Demetrius by Plutarch. Seleucus I, ruler of a large empire in Asia minor, was married to Stratonike. Antiochus, his son from a first wife, secretly in love with his stepmother, falls ill. The cause of that sickness remains a mystery until the physician is finally able to determine its nature when he notices that as soon as Stratonike enters Antiochus's room, his pulse beat becomes irregular. In a ruse, the physician tells the king that Antiochus is secretly in love with his, that is the physician's, wife. When Seleucus tells him that he must give her up, the physician reveals the true object of Antiochus's longing, and the king magnanimously cedes Stratonike to his son.

The story became a favorite topic for a great number of painters of the seventeenth and eighteenth centuries. There have been several suggestions as to which specific painting Goethe had in mind. For my purpose, though, only the information given in the text is of importance.[1]

I could demonstrate the fascinating manner in which Goethe brings out different aspects of the painting of the sick prince in a way that parallels Wilhelm's own development. As I have shown elsewhere, he projects his feelings on to the characters of the painting and on to their interrelationship as the scene depicted suggests.[2] Here I want to emphasize that Wilhelm's looking at the painting, at Antiochus and Stratonike, implies prophetic anticipation of his own development, and that Stratonike's role in the painting foreshadows that of Natalie, the woman with whom Wilhelm will ultimately be united.

There is one further matter that needs to be mentioned before proceeding. The importance of the painting of the sick prince is evident from the fact that it was added to the first, fragmentary version of the novel, entitled *Wilhelm Meisters theatralische Sendung* [not published until 1885; Wilhelm Meister's Theatrical Mission]. Neither the painting nor the art collection to which it belongs nor the persons who connect Wilhelm to the painting were in the earlier version. Missing was Natalie and her family who play such an important role in the last three books, that is, in those parts of the *Lehrjahre* that had no counterpart in the fragment.

My point of departure is a passage in book four. Wilhelm had been elected leader of a small group of actors. They had performed at a castle and had been generously compensated for their efforts. Wilhelm persuades the others to disregard rumors about a small military unit that might pose a threat to them if they were to take the planned route. While resting in a field they are attacked, robbed of most of their belongings, and several of them who tried to offer resistance are wounded. Wilhelm's wound is the most serious. While he is lying on the ground, a group of riders approaches, led by a woman on a white horse. She shows great concern about Wilhelm's well-being and orders the surgeon, who is among those accompanying her, to attend to his wound. Wilhelm is amazed by her nobility and overhears her telling her uncle — as she addresses him — that it is on their account that he is suffering, a remark he cannot understand. Only much later does he find out that the attackers had wanted to rob the group of noblemen but had mistakenly attacked the actors. The noble woman — only at the end of the novel does Wilhelm learn her name, Natalie — had borrowed her uncle's coat because of the cool evening air. She now uses it to cover Wilhelm to protect him from the elements. Wilhelm admires her beautiful figure when the surgeon touches his wound to extract the bullet that is lodged in his flesh. In a vision Wilhelm sees her head surrounded by beams of light and her entire figure bathed in a bright glow; then he passes out. The "holy one" (die Heilige), as he calls her, and her party proceed on their way, leaving the surgeon behind.

Wilhelm is placed in the care of a minister so that he can recover. While convalescing he again and again remembers the scene in which the beautiful Amazon, his name for Natalie, comes to his side and takes off her coat. It is clearly a very special moment that is singled out by an unusual vocabulary. We find words like "Ritter" [knight], "Wahlplatz" [place of military encounter], "ihr Haupt mit Strahlen umgeben" [her head surrounded by beams of light], and the already mentioned "Heilige." One could call it an epiphany, a stepping into this world of something sacred, that is, the very special woman in Wilhelm's life. In his mind he connects the scene in the field where the beautiful Samaritan and the surgeon come to his rescue with the painting of the sick prince in which the physician is at the prince's bedside and the concerned princess approaches him. Wilhelm wonders:

> Sollten nicht [. . .] uns in der Jugend wie im Schlafe, die Bilder zukünftiger Schicksale umschweben, und unserm unbefangenen Auge ahnungsvoll sichtbar werden?[3]

Here we have an excellent statement on what I mean by prophetic vision, a vision that in Wilhelm's mind is associated with the ability of the youthful eye to divine the pictures that make up our future. Wilhelm continues by asking himself:

> [. . .] sollten die Keime dessen, was uns begegnen wird, nicht schon von der Hand des Schicksals ausgestreut, sollte nicht ein Vorgenuß der Früchte, die wir einst zu brechen hoffen, möglich sein?[4] (IV, 9)

Wilhelm, as later on the protagonist of Eduard Mörike's *Maler Nolten* [Painter Nolten], a novel I will take up below, sees his future as already determined by fate.

I must now explain how Wilhelm came to know the painting of the sick prince. He first saw it in his grandfather's collection when he was a child. When the grandfather died, the collection was put up for sale; a person called the Abbé, an agent for a wealthy nobleman, evaluated the collection and found the amount the heir wanted for it reasonable. Thus, the collection came into possession of Natalie's uncle, that is, into the possession of the man who accompanied the woman Wilhelm saw dismount from the white horse and who then saw to it that he was taken care of when lying wounded on the ground. Natalie will, after her uncle's death, inherit that collection. Thus, one can talk of a "homecoming" for Wilhelm — Thomas P. Saine's felicitous phrase[5]—when he is united with her and the works of art at the end of the novel.

I must return to the time when the Abbé first met Wilhelm whom the Abbé got to know when he evaluated the art collection of Wilhelm's grandfather. It must have been on account of the impression Wilhelm made on the Abbé that he selected the boy as a good prospect for membership in the *Turmgesellschaft*, the Society of the Tower, a loosely connected group of mostly well-to-do aristocrats, with the Abbé as their adviser. He notices that Wilhelm has a favorite painting in the collection, the one of the sick prince. When the two meet again, years later, but before Wilhelm's encounter with Natalie, their conversation turns to the painting. Wilhelm still esteems it highly even though they both agree that it is not an especially outstanding work of art in comparison to other pieces in the collection. It is the subject matter that attracted him when he was a child and that still attracts him now that he is a young man. The child's identification with the prince of the painting clearly points to the classical Freudian prototypical relationship between son and parents. Wilhelm will find ultimately in Natalie, who is prefigured as the Stratonike of the painting, the ideal mother for his child from another woman. There is in both the narrative and in the painting the healing figure of the physician. One must see, then, Wilhelm's development as a normal one of growing out of the mother fixation at the time when he was a child to relationships with women of his own age. Still, there is in his identification with the sick prince also the element of prophetic vision in the sense that Stratonike stands for both Wilhelm's mother and the object of his desires, as well as, later on, the mother for his child.

I want to return to the part of the novel where Wilhelm is recovering from his wound. He is trying desperately to find out the identity of the noble family that came to his rescue, but his search is in vain. After many adventures and after having been initiated into the Society of the Tower, Wilhelm believes that Therese, the owner and most admirable administrator of a small estate, would make a good mother for his son Felix. They get engaged. However, when he afterwards again meets Natalie, he realizes that he made a terrible mistake. He becomes an irritable, socially impossible person, a "sick" man. Natalie's younger brother Friedrich, the black sheep of the family but also the one who has the best sense of humor, overhears Natalie's confession of love for Wilhelm. Friedrich then points to the painting of the sick prince and tells how the physician finally hit upon the true cause of the prince's sickness and how he now can prescribe a medicine that tastes as good as it is beneficial. With his humorous speech Friedrich brings out into the open Natalie's and Wilhelm's love for each other.

The heading of this chapter, "Prophetic Vision," thus fits Goethe's use of the painting of the sick prince. The child Wilhelm, by selecting the painting as his favorite, empathizes with the prince and thus recognizes his own rather passive character. When he is at an impasse as to how to solve the dilemma that he is engaged to Therese but in love with Natalie, the family's physician declares him to be sick and his friend Friedrich has to break the ice and solve the problem to everybody's satisfaction. Such passivity has been evident in a number of situations of the novel. As Stratonike comes to the ailing prince in the painting, Natalie comes to the help of the wounded Wilhelm and as the prince will be united with Stratonike, Wilhelm will be united with Natalie at the end of the novel after others have solved his dilemma.

There is one more interesting aspect that connects the painting of the sick prince with the narrative and with Lessing's aesthetic theory as he explained it in *Laokoon*. As I mentioned in chapter one, in discussing the Laocoon group Lessing develops the idea that the depiction of the moment before the climax of an action has the greatest effect since a viewer can then supply the subsequent action in his/her own imagination. That imagination surpasses any attempt by the artist to depict the climax. Also, if the artist shows the climactic moment, there is necessarily a letdown as far as the viewer's imagination is concerned.

The painting of the sick prince fulfills Lessing's principle perfectly. We witness the moment before the physician's revelation of the true cause for the prince's sickness and before the various consequences that revelation will bring about. Goethe knew Lessing's essay and wrote on the Laocoon group himself ("Über Laokoon"; 1798). Readers of the *Lehrjahre* have at times wondered about whether Natalie and Wilhelm will actually get married since there is no definite proof for such an event in the text. I relate Goethe's decision to end the narrative just before the traditional climax, that is, the wedding of the protagonists, to the Laocoon principle.

In the preceding pages I have tried to show how Wilhelm, when first viewing the painting of the sick prince, has anticipated in the figure of Stratonike his own Natalie. Neither in the painting nor in the text are we presented with the fulfillment of the joining in marriage of the two couples in love, but only with the moment before. As a child Wilhelm visualizes a mother figure as the object of his desires but not as something actually possessed. Thus, the painting of the sick prince corresponds so closely to his subconscious. When that figure gains reality in the form of Natalie, the fulfillment of what Stratonike of the painting has prefigured and promised, has come a step closer. The final step, though, will be taken in the reader's imagination.

Mörike: *Maler Nolten*

In both Goethe's *Wilhelm Meisters Lehrjahre* and Eduard Mörike's *Maler Nolten. Eine Novelle in zwei Teilen* [1832; Painter Nolten. A Novella in Two Parts] the action is repeatedly interrupted by retrospective accounts. Thus, in the *Lehrjahre* Wilhelm's first encounter with the painting of the sick prince precedes the beginning of the novel by a long time but we hear about it at the end of the first book. In the case of *Maler Nolten* the various time frames are intermixed in such a way as to make it virtually impossible for the reader to reconstruct a rectilinear sequence of events. There are three important paintings in Mörike's novel (the term novella used in the title is misleading). Their origin precedes the beginning of the novel, one of the paintings even goes back to about the time of the protagonist's, that is, Theobald Nolten's birth. In *Maler Nolten,* again as in the *Lehrjahre,* the narrative movement is directed not only toward the past but toward the future. Critics have pointed out many such passages; here I want to concentrate on the prophetic vision evident in two sketches that Theobald drew and in which a woman is the central object.

The plot of *Maler Nolten* goes back to the protagonist's uncle, Friedrich Nolten, a painter, who on a trip to Bohemia ends up one night alone and lost in the woods. He finds refuge with a band of gypsies among whom the beautiful and enigmatic Loskine exerts an irresistible attraction upon him. They separate from the band, marry, and have a daughter whom they name Elisabeth. The mother dies at childbirth. At age seven Elisabeth runs away from her father and from then on leads a nomadic life. The memory of Loskine is kept alive through a portrait Friedrich Nolten had made of her. He disappeared and afterwards the portrait is stored in his brother's attic where the young Theobald, Friedrich's nephew, discovers it. He is mesmerized by the woman portrayed, and she becomes an idol for him. At age sixteen, on an excursion with an older sister, Theobald meets the living double of the woman of the portrait: it is Elisabeth who looks exactly like her mother. Upon hearing her sing and then seeing her, Theobald loses consciousness. After having been revived by Elisabeth, Theobald tells her of the sensation he had when fainting, a sensation that seemed to make him reach the bottom depth of his psyche and the earliest stage of his existence. When he woke up, he tells Elisabeth, he looked into her eyes as if into a bottomless well in which the secret of his life could be found. The two make a vow of spiritual union, a vow that Elisabeth keeps until her death. In her eyes Theobald belongs to her; she scares away rivals and tries to reach him with unrelenting determination, braving any number of obstacles. The encounter with Elisabeth also means for Theobald the decision to devote his life to painting. We learn from various characters that elves and other spirits have been a favorite of his since early childhood. The fateful encounter with Elisabeth and his preoccupation with spirits will be reflected in two sketches he drew in which a woman is the central object. They are introduced in a long description at the beginning of the novel and give evidence of his prophetic vision in that they foreshadow important aspects of his own life.

Before I turn to the contents of the two paintings, I must briefly explain their origin. They go back to pencil and chalk sketches that Theobald drew and that fell into the hands of a painter named Tillsen who executed one of them in oil, the other in water color. A friend and benefactor of Tillsen has seen the two paintings at the house of an acquaintance and rushes to congratulate Tillsen on having achieved a breakthrough in his art. The painter is reluctant to admit his authorship, which prompts the visitor to give him — and, more important, the reader — a detailed description of the paintings. Obviously, Mörike wanted to introduce the works of art at the beginning of the novel and was unable to find a less obtrusive way to do just that. The length of the descriptions contrasts sharply with the few sentences Goethe used to mention the painting of the sick prince at the end of book one of the *Lehrjahre*. That length also violates Lessing's well-argued admonition in *Laokoon* to avoid the description of static situations.

The first painting is a seascape with a nymph on the left who is half submerged in the water. Her face is that of Elisabeth and she is singing. While the boy is attracted by the magic of the nymph's voice and instinctively ("unwillkürlich") stretches out his arm toward her, he is also frightened by her and pulls back. Just as interesting is the imposing figure of the satyr who is leaning on an oar and responsible for handing over the youth to the nymph. The person describing the scene claims to know that the satyr had stolen the youth. While the satyr thus wants to do a favor to the nymph, he is at the same time overcome by jealousy.

The second painting, as I said above, again based on a sketch by Theobald, points clearly in the direction of the ending of the novel, that is, the death of the four protagonists: Theobald, Elisabeth, Agnes, the girl Theobald wanted to marry, and his close friend Larkens. The painting is a nightly ghost scene, populated with skeletons who have momentarily escaped their nearby tombs. The scene is again dominated by Elisabeth, this time playing an organ. According to the narrator, she seems to be no longer concerned with matters of this world in which she has participated for a while but is already dreamily thinking of a return to another, better world. Death is shown working in the bellows, while half-dressed skeletons are either engaged in a solemn, even sad dance or in frolicking games.

It is relatively easy to see how Theobald's state of mind is reflected in the first sketch. His creative imagination has made Elisabeth into a nymph who lures men to follow her into the carefree existence under water — a well-known traditional theme in literature. Theobald expresses on various occasions that his life is governed by forces beyond his control; thus the fact that the youth in the sketch is being handed over to the nymph is a fitting depiction of that feeling. His stretching out his hand toward her instinctively shows how deeply attracted Theobald is to her, his feeling of repulsion reflects the danger he knows Elisabeth poses. The nymph's singing agrees of course with the singing of Elisabeth when she and Theobald first met. Just as dominant as Elisabeth is in the first sketch so she is in the second in which she plays the organ. Here she presides over a night scene of ghostly skeletons who have escaped temporarily from their tombs. In Theobald's mind, on the conscious or subconscious level, Elisabeth is associated with death and the entry into a nonhuman, blissful existence. Thus, some of the dancers are solemn and sad reflecting the artist's realization of what it means to lose one's life. Others, though, are frolicking around and engaged in humorous games and thus give expression to that new, careless existence beyond death. The second sketch prefigures eerily the ending of the novel when Theobald is at a castle and believes one night to hear Elisabeth play an organ in one of the rooms. In a truly spooky ending a blind gardener discovers in that moment the dead Theobald, but then soon afterwards sees Elisabeth and Theobald as shades, him following her, leave the room. While Theobald's shade does not pay any attention to his dead double, his face shows a pitiful expression when he sees the gardener. Theobald has here again depicted his ambivalent feelings toward Elisabeth, who is his angel of death.

In *Maler Nolten* we have, then, an artist who expresses in two sketches the impact upon him of the coming together of the idolized woman of the portrait in his father's attic and the living double of that woman. Theobald's artistic creativity converts the impact of the encounter into two scenes that bring out areas of his psyche that lie below the surface of his consciousness and thus reach essential aspects of his personality, aspects that will come to the fore in his life. Central to that life is his relationship to Elisabeth, and it is Elisabeth who has the dominant role both in the sketches and in his life.

Theobald's prophetic vision is certainly at work in the two sketches on which Tillsen's paintings are based.[6] The sketches and the paintings based on them thus belong to the realistic aspects of the novel. Interpreters have pointed to psychological realism as the best approach to *Maler Nolten*. However, the working of fate has also been mentioned as underlying important aspects of the novel. Another look at the sketches will shed light on the issue of the two possible approaches to the text, the one focusing on its psychological realism and the one stressing supernatural forces.[7]

Mörike, as mentioned above, arranged the sequence of events in *Maler Nolten* in a most intricate pattern. As a consequence, readers are often in the dark as to the cause and effect connection between events. They will thus see the apparent working of fate in the lives of various characters. Readers will find confirmation of their impression that fate plays an important role when they notice the many mentionings of intuitive actions and of prophecies or when they read the beautiful poem "Der Feuerreiter" (The Fire Rider) in which the rider seems to anticipate with his ride through town, the outbreak of a fire. Some of the characters, especially Theobald himself, make no secret of their conviction that their lives are governed by fate. When we read about the contents of the two sketches and then notice how various aspects are realized in the course of the narrative, especially how Elisabeth plays the organ both in the sketch and when Theobald dies, we tend to make fate responsible for the anticipatory quality of his works. The same is true of the figure of the satyr who seems to anticipate Theobald's friend Larkens, a comic actor who has a strong influence on Theobald while they are at the court. The reader's impression of the prophetic, rationally inexplicable, quality of some details of Theobald's two sketches reinforces, then, other aspects of the novel that point towards fate as a governing force.

However, upon closer scrutiny one realizes that these anticipatory details do go not beyond the psychological possible. Theobald might well have come up with a satyr as the equivalent of a future, influential person in his life, choosing that particular creature since it blends in well with the nymph, that is, with Elisabeth. It is true that Theobald could in no way have foreseen that there would be in his life an actor friend. However, the satyr's handing over the youth, that is, Theobald, to the nymph does not prefigure what actually happens. Larkens is instrumental in getting Theobald back with Agnes whom Theobald knew when she was still a child and whom he wanted to marry before he met Constanze, a lady at the court. For those who think that psychological realism is the best approach to *Maler Nolten*, the ending of the novel proves to be most difficult to explain. Here the blind gardener claims he has seen Elisabeth and Theobald as shades who pass by the dead Theobald. That ending parallels the equally ambiguous one of Goethe's *Wahlverwandtschaften* [Elective Affinities] when Ottilie's body is carried through the street to be buried, and Nanni, a girl very much devoted to Ottilie, throws herself from the loft of a house onto the street when the funeral procession passes by. When the coffin bearers lift up the seemingly dead Nanni so that she touches Ottilie's gown and hands, Nanni comes back to life.

That Mörike was intent on providing realistic explanations for the events of the novel can be seen in the following rather odd detail. Elisabeth, as I mentioned above, is jealous of the two women who are rivals in her claim on Theobald. In order to show that Constanze, one of the two rivals, recognizes Elisabeth from a distance in the street, the narrator makes the comment that Constanze, who had never met Elisabeth before, identifies her correctly as the organist in Tillsen's painting. To make such a recognition more plausible, Mörike has the narrator mention that Theobald had touched up the organist's face in Tillsen's painting so as to make it resemble Elisabeth as much as possible.[8] It is far-fetched to have one artist go over the work of another in this way. Only Mörike's desire to give rational explanations for the events of the novel — here Constanze's recognition of Elisabeth from a painting — could have motivated him to add this unconvincing detail.

Ultimately, the two paintings described at the beginning of *Maler Nolten* are to be considered examples of works of art that give evidence of prophetic vision. For me they are the product of Theobald's ability to reach in his art deep layers of his psyche. These layers are intimately connected with the essence of his personality and thus also with his future life and art.

Maler Nolten, as must be clear to the reader by now, is a strange work that resists clear-cut interpretation. One enigmatic aspect pertains at least peripherally to the general topic of this book and will, therefore, be discussed here.

It will be remembered that the portrait of Loskine, the gypsy wife of Friedrich Nolten, was stored in the attic of his nephew's, that is, of Theobald's house. Everybody assumed that Friedrich had died, but in the concluding paragraphs of the novel we learn that he is still alive and that he had lived at the same court where Theobald was. The uncle had been several times at the point of revealing himself to the nephew before the latter went away. Friedrich's life is at one point said to be the prototype of that of his nephew Theobald whom the uncle calls his second "I." We must then ask why Friedrich survives his encounter with Loskine while his nephew must die with her daughter, with Elisabeth. Of course, one could say that Loskine had died soon after she and the uncle were married while Elisabeth keeps pursuing Theobald until his death. Still, one must ask why did the author have Friedrich first presumed dead and then, in the last paragraph of the novel, reappear alive. The only possible explanation I can find is that Friedrich was able to complete a portrait of Loskine before giving up painting. He was able to convert his obsession with the gypsy into a finished portrait and thus had come to terms with that part of his life. Theobald, on the other hand, had not been able to complete Elisabeth's portraits. All he accomplished were two sketches that Tillsen will be most impressed by but about which he will say that the drawing showed a number of deficiencies ("manche Mängel an der Zeichnung").[9] Theobald is destined never to come to a resolution as to his relationship to Elisabeth and thus must die.

At the beginning of his journey there was the fateful encounter with the portrait of Loskine/Elisabeth under whose mysterious power Theobald was to come for the rest of his life. A man's gaze at the artistic rendering of a woman was in *Maler Nolten* to determine the protagonist's destiny.

When we look back at the two instances of prophetic vision in connection with the two novels, we notice marked differences in the way Goethe and Mörike introduce the paintings. In *Wilhelm Meisters Lehrjahre* the young Wilhelm has selected in his grandfather's collection a painting that shows a woman coming toward a young man lying in bed. Here we have a clear anticipation of Natalie's caring nature, that is, of the woman with whom Wilhelm will be united at the end of the novel. In Mörike's *Maler Nolten* there is the fateful portrait of Loskine to which Theobald is magically drawn. Then there is his meeting her double, her daughter Elisabeth, who will dominate Theobald's life and art. Two sketches of his, used by another artist, are described at the beginning of the novel. In them a woman, clearly recognizable as Elisabeth, and other figures and objects point toward the resolution of the novel. Thus, while the ways the various paintings are introduced differ sharply, the painting of the sick prince in Goethe's novel and the two sketches in Mörike's novel share the function of prophesying the protagonist's future, specifically Wilhelm's and Theobald's future in relationship to the key women in their lives.

Notes

[1] There is an excellent summary of the significance of the "Painting of the Sick Prince" for the *Lehrjahre* in section I, volume 9, of Johann Wolfgang Goethe, *Sämtliche Werke, Briefe, Tagebücher und Gespräche* (Frankfurt/Main: Deutscher Klassiker Verlag, 1992), 1395–98. The summary also contains a bibliography of pertinent studies.

[2] Christoph E. Schweitzer, "Wilhelm Meister und das Bild vom kranken Königssohn," *PMLA* 72 (1957), 419–32.

[3] [Whether the pictures of our future destiny . . . should not hover around us when we are young, as in sleep, and whether these pictures should not become visible to our uncluttered eye as in a premonition?]

[4] [Whether it isn't possible that the hand of fate had already spread the seeds of what will happen to us and whether it is not possible that we can have a foretaste of the fruits that we hope to enjoy some day?]

[5] Thomas P. Saine, "Wilhelm Meister's Homecoming," *JEGPh* 69 (1970). 450–69.

[6] Bernard Dieterle, who refers to only one of the two paintings, that is, to the night scene with the organ player, is the latest critic to point to its prophetic function. However, his approach and that of the preceding critics differ radically from mine (Bernard Dieterle, *Erzählte Bilder. Zum narrativen Umgang mit Gemälden,* [Marburg: Hitzeroth, 1988], 109, 110, 115).

[7] Here I will consider primarily the role the two paintings play in showing the best approach to the sequence of events. For a general discussion of the issue, see for instance Jeffrey L. Sammons, "Fate and Psychology: Another Look at Mörike's *Maler Nolten,*" *Lebendige Form. Interpretationen zur deutschen Literatur. Festschrift für Heinrich E. K. Henel,* ed. Jeffrey L. Sammons and Ernst Schürer (Munich: Wilhelm Fink, 1970), 211–27, especially 224–6.

[8] "Er hatte, wie der Leser weiß, in der Skizze, die bei dem Gemälde zu Grunde gelegen, jene Wahnsinnige kenntlich genug gezeichnet, ja er hatte noch auf Tillsens ausgeführtem Tableau dem merkwürdigen Kopfe durch wenig beigefügte Striche die äußerste Ähnlichkeit gegeben." [He had, as the reader knows, drawn the insane woman [Elisabeth] on the sketch that formed the model for the painting so that she was easily recognizable. What is more, he had on Tillsen's completed tableau made her striking head even more lifelike by adding a few strokes of the brush.] Eduard Mörike, *Werke und Briefe.* Vol. 3. *Maler Nolten* (Stuttgart: Klett, 1967), 256–7.

[9] P. 18 in the edition of Mörike's *Werke und Briefe* referred to in note 8.

4: Seeing and Not Seeing: The Visual Image as Displacement

Hauff: *Die Bettlerin vom Pont des Arts*

In Wilhem Hauff's *Die Bettlerin vom Pont des Arts* [1836; The Beggar Woman of the Pont des Arts] and in Wilhelm Jensen's *Gradiva. Ein pompejanisches Phantasiestück* [1903; Gradiva. A Fantastic Pompeian Story] we have two novellas in which the protagonist has transferred the attraction he feels for a beloved living woman to a work of art. In each story the art object serves as a replacement to such a degree that the live beloved has to take special steps to make the protagonist see that she, not her artistic double, is really the one he has had in mind all the time. The process of transfer and delusion is worked out in much more detail in Jensen's *Gradiva* than in the Hauff novella.

Hauff's story combines truly romantic aspects with equally interesting realistic features. Among the romantic aspects we have Fröben, the protagonist, falling in love at first sight, his faithfulness to a practically unknown woman whom in all probability he will never meet again, his meeting up with her double as a painting by Lucas Cranach, the Elder, a painting that is some three hundreds years old, and his meeting her again as the wife of a close friend, Faldner. Add to that his encounter in front of the Cranach painting with another admirer of the woman portrayed and Hauff's debt to the romantic tradition, in this case especially to E. T. A. Hoffmann and his many coincidental happenings, is clearly illustrated. As is well known, Hoffmann uses paintings again and again to establish surprising encounters between viewers and their past.

But there are equally important aspects of Hauff's novella that point toward realism. While the information about the exact year in which the action proper begins and the detailed description of specific areas in both Paris and Stuttgart have their equivalents in stories by Hoffmann, see for instance his *Die Fermate* which I will take up in chapter VI, his friend Faldner is drawn with realistic sharpness: he is the know-it-all, never-satisfied man who is always critical of those dependent on him but afraid of the judgment of his equals. Also realistic is the description of the way Faldner treats his wife, Josephe, whom he married so as to exploit her as a household servant to whom he could give orders. She turns out to be the "beggar woman of the Pont des Arts," with whom Fröben fell in love in Paris and could not forget. The novella ends with the separation of Faldner and Josephe, who as a Catholic is unable to remarry but who converts to Protestantism so as to marry Fröben.

When Fröben first saw Josephe standing on the bridge in Paris, she was a beggar whom his friend Faldner took to be a common prostitute. It is night when they meet her. They cannot see her face because she wears a mask. Fröben senses something special in her manner and speech. They can converse in German since, as we learn in the course of the story, her father was from the German-speaking part of Switzerland. Fröben tries in vain to persuade her to let him see her face. All he achieves is that she accepts his money — she needs it for her sick mother — and that she promises him to be back a week later. At that time he engages her to embroider some handkerchiefs that he cleverly brought along so as to be able both to continue seeing her and also to help her financially. Finally, Fröben has to leave Paris. He obtains permission to visit her and her mother at which time she uncovers most of her face and they kiss. Fröben makes Josephe promise to be back at the Pont des Arts at their usual place and time a month hence when he is to be back from his trip. He waits in vain for her, and disconsolate he returns to Germany. In Stuttgart, as mentioned above, he finds in a gallery the beloved's portrait in a painting by Lucas Cranach. It is an exact likeness except for the clothing. Fröben makes a daily pilgrimage to the painting and meets there on *his* daily pilgrimage a Spanish nobleman who is just as certain as Fröben is that Cranach's painting is a portrait of his, the Spaniards, former beloved. It turns out, as we learn later, that we have here a case of mother/daughter likeness, that Fröben's Josephe is the daughter of the Spaniard's beloved of some twenty years ago. The mother had run away with a handsome Swiss soldier, Josephe's father. Fröben cannot bring himself to leave Stuttgart until he is given a lithograph copy of the Cranach painting.

Fröben then visits his friend Faldner who lives on an estate in the beautiful Rhine valley near Kaub. Josephe now married to Faldner thinks that she recognizes in Fröben's voice the one she heard in Paris belonging to her benefactor but quickly dismisses the thought as utterly fantastic. Also, by her marriage to Faldner she has been "unfaithful" to the man she had fallen in love with in Paris. How could she now face up to him? Fröben is strongly attracted to Josephe and feels more and more disgust toward Faldner who turns out to be an insufferable human being and an even more impossible, fault-finding, arrogant husband. When Fröben retires to his room in the evening, he pulls out the copy of the Cranach painting and is struck by the resemblance between it and Josephe. But he also accuses himself of becoming unfaithful to the beloved, to the beggar woman of the Pont des Arts. The portrait has taken the place of the beloved to such a degree "daß er die Unbekannte sich nicht mehr anders dachte als wie dieses Bild"[1] [that he couldn't imagine the unknown one in any way other than as this picture]. Later on he will tell her that she resembled "jenem Bilde, das ich durch einen wahrhaftigen Kreislauf der Dinge als dir ähnlich gefunden und geliebt hatte"[2] [that picture which, because of a truly circular movement of things, I found to resemble you and loved].

Fröben turns once more to Cranach's portrait after having told the story of his encounter with the beggar woman in Paris to a group of guests at Faldner's house. Faldner had been looking forward to a salacious account of Fröben's affair with a prostitute and makes no secret of his idea of what really must have happened between the two. Josephe, as a result of her husband's innuendoes, faints and has to be taken to her room. Fröben retires and, while looking at Cranach's portrait, chides himself for having revealed to strangers the story of his love, to have spoken to them about the beauty and purity of the woman of the portrait.

Josephe, now that she feels that her husband has gone beyond the limits of her endurance and also with the certainty that Fröben is the beloved benefactor from Paris who has remained faithful to her, begins to make him aware of the fact that she is the beggar woman. She does this by approaching him, while he is asleep in an arbor in the garden, in the same costume she wore when they met on the Pont des Arts and by leaving tell-tale signs: the ring he had given her then and a handkerchief he had asked her to embroider. This is when

Fröben feels that he is betraying the woman of Cranach's portrait which has taken the place of the real person. It takes some rather strong measures on Josephe's part to have Fröben see that his friend's wife is the beloved beggar woman. In the process he thinks that he must have dreamed all that he has been noticing or that he must have lost his mind. He dreams of the beggar woman who turns into the Spaniard he met at the gallery, then he is in that gallery in Stuttgart where the paintings had been rearranged so that he cannot find the Cranach portrait. When he begins to call out loud in despair, the guard admonishes him to be quiet so as not to wake the paintings that are asleep now. When he finally finds the portrait, it has changed to a full-size representation of the beloved who steps out of the frame toward him. Now, while he is between dreaming and being awake, Josephe kisses him. Still believing that he is really dreaming, he sees the beggar woman disappear. Hauff clearly shows in this scene the circular movement of the story. We proceed from the live beggar woman who, as she had stepped out of the painting, now steps into the dream and then almost into the waking reality of Fröben's mind.

Fröben cannot explain rationally the visions he had of the beggar woman nor the objects he found next to him when he woke up from his slumber, objects he knows could only come from the beggar woman. The gardener, whom Fröben asks about the identity of the person he suspects of having left ring and handkerchief next to him on the bench, believes Fröben to be mentally unbalanced. It is Josephe's second approach to the slumbering Fröben that brings about his waking up while she is kissing him and thus his discovery that Josephe, his friend's wife, is the beggar woman of the Pont des Arts.

All ends well: Faldner agrees to a separation — a beggar woman could not possibly be his wife after all. Josephe converts to Protestantism and thus, having obtained the divorce, can marry Fröben. To underscore the importance of the Cranach portrait for the story, Hauff has Josephe wear in the last scene an exact replica of the clothing as well as of the heavy jewelry the woman wears in Cranach's painting. Thus she tells Fröben that the living beloved and the woman of the painting, who had displaced the real person and to whom Fröben had transferred his affection, are one and the same.

Even though the process of displacement, transfer, and delusion are handled in a masterful way in Hauff's novella, we will see a much more detailed and psychologically insightful elaboration in Wilhelm Jensen's *Gradiva. Ein pompejanisches Phantasiestück.*[3]

Jensen: *Gradiva. Ein pompejanisches Phantasiestück*

There are strong similarities between Hauff's *Die Bettlerin vom Pont des Arts* and Wilhelm Jensen's *Gradiva. Ein pompejanisches Phantasiestück.* [1903; Gradiva; A Fantastic Pompeian Story], especially in connection with a work of art that displaces the beloved woman. Jensen has worked out the psychological phases of transfer, delusion, and the gradual redirection toward sanity of the protagonist with great insight and fascinating detail. It comes, then, as no surprise that *Gradiva* attracted Sigmund Freud to such an extent that he devoted his first major literary analysis to it.[4] The following observation will make clear Freud's reasons for seeing in the story evidence of the depiction of processes that were also being described by him in his various psychoanalytic publications. Freud's interest in the story is also easily understood by Jensen's reproduction of the protagonist's revealing dreams. In addition, given Freud's well-known love of classical artifacts, the fact that Jensen's protagonist is an archeologist who in the course of the action decides to go to Italy and ends up in Pompeii adds to the attraction *Gradiva* had for Freud. Here I want to focus on the role the work of art plays in the story and how there is, as we had observed in the case of Hauff, a circular movement, first away from the living person and toward the art object, and then back again to the person.

The plot of *Gradiva* is relatively simple. Norbert Hanold and Zoë Bertgang liked each other as teenagers. He took to archeology and became oblivious to anything but his studies. In Rome he sees the relief of a young woman from antiquity and is immediately attracted to the work. He is especially intrigued by the vertical position of her right foot. Since she is stepping forward, he calls her "Gradiva." Norbert is delighted to be able to obtain a plaster cast that he mounts on a wall in his apartment in Germany, where he studies it daily. In all of this he does not realize nor does the author tell the reader that underneath the fascination with "Gradiva" lies his repressed desire for Zoë Bertgang, the "gang" (walk) part of her name emerging as "Gradiva." Also, his subconscious has found a duplicate in the relief of Zoë's peculiar lifting of her feet when walking. In the streets in front of the apartment he tries to ascertain whether "Gradiva's" vertical positioning of her feet is physically possible and makes a fool of himself with his investigations. Norbert becomes more and more a man controlled by his internal drives. He is clearly a sexually repressed person whose subconscious makes him do things for whose justification he has to go to great lengths.

In Hauff's story we had a dream in which the work of art, that is, Cranach's painting, came alive. The same happens in Jensen's story: Norbert dreams about "Gradiva" who appears alive among the ruins of Pompeii. He also identifies with a caged canary in an open window near his apartment: he imagines that the bird is yearning to be set free. Being financially independent and thus free to do what he pleases, he decides on the spur of the moment to go to Italy. In Italy he ends up in Pompeii where, for the first time since the beginning of his studies, he feels a deep dissatisfaction with his profession as being utterly useless. In the heat of midday and full of strange ideas about the possibility of the prototype of "Gradiva" having lived and perished in Pompeii, he finds himself in one of the houses of the city and suddenly sees what he comes to call the "Gradiva rediviva." He does not know whether he is fantasizing or whether the figure belongs to this world. As it turns out, it is actually Zoë Bertgang who is in Pompeii with her father, an entomologist. While he is trying to capture live insects, she is trying to recapture Norbert's interest that she lost when he turned to study archeology. She wears the clothing of the woman of the relief, has, as already mentioned, the same facial features, and raises, when walking, her feet in a 180 degree angle. She is clever enough to appear to Norbert in the right places and at the most propitious moments. When he first sees her, she doesn't give him time to react and talk to her but disappears quickly to what his delusion believes to be Hades.

From here on Jensen has Zoë bring Norbert back from his delusion to the reality of herself and the world around them. She does this in an impressive manner, being at first taken aback by and annoyed at the extreme nature of his deluded mind, when, among other strange manifestations he addresses her first in Greek, then in Latin, neither language she understands. Gradually she comes to have pity for his derangement, understands the nature of his delusion, and, impersonating the classical "Gradiva," leads him to the "real" Zoë, to herself. Freud was obviously impressed by her, that is,

Jensen's insights into a mind like Norbert's and by her careful way of guiding him back to sanity. She shows clear superiority in this undertaking, at times hardly able to suppress an expression of mockery at the apparent silliness of some of his statements and actions. Finally, when he is about cured of his illusion, she tells him the truth, explaining the transfer of his affection for her to "Gradiva." She then tells him how she happened to be in Pompeii and how, after meeting with him in one of the houses of the city, she learned to take up the role of the classical "Gradiva."

Josephe in Hauff's *Die Bettlerin vom Pont des Arts* had duplicated the clothing of the woman of Cranach's painting in the last scene of the story and had thus told Fröben that she is the real focus of his attention not her double as a work of art. Zoë in Jensen's *Gradiva* duplicates, as we have seen, the clothing of the woman of the classical relief. At the end of the story the author shows how much Norbert has understood the subconscious transfer of his fixation with Zoë's walk, really a case of fetishism, to the relief where the woman is shown with the same peculiarity: in the last scene of the novella Norbert asks Zoë to walk in front of him so that he can observe in the living beloved the special feature that he had subconsciously transferred from her to the relief and now consciously notices in Zoë Bertgang's walk. Thus the movement from life to art and now back to life has come full circle and life and love have won out. As a humorous addition, Norbert sees at one point, when he has already been cured, a dimple in Zoë's face, thus receiving confirmation for his newly found discovery that she is his teenage playmate and not "Gradiva": he knows that the woman of the relief does not have a dimple.

There are other aspects that show similarities between the novella by Hauff and the one by Jensen. In both the men first *see* the woman, *see* her duplicate as work of art, and finally *see* the real woman behind the work of art. Their interest in and desire for the woman is clearly aroused by her physical appearance. In this respect the transfer of the living woman to a work of art speaks for itself: the woman as art is the passive object of the man's gaze. Not so in the case of the two women. We never read about Josephe's impression of Fröben's appearance, nor of Zoë's impression of Norbert's. Josephe is obviously taken by Fröben's decency and his charitable actions when they meet on the bridge in Paris, and, interestingly enough, thinks she recognizes him by his voice when he visits Faldner, Josephe's husband. Zoë liked Norbert as a teenager and tried in vain to keep him interested in her at various parties to which they went but where he was completely disinterested in anything social and thus also oblivious of her presence. As she tells him at the end, he didn't so much as notice or see her. She never mentions his appearance but seems to feel that behind his all-encompassing devotion to archeology lies a warm human being that needs help and that she could live with. Both authors thus emphasize the male gaze and the visual stimulus as being the primary agents for the male's becoming interested in and desirous of a woman. An extreme case occurs when that gaze focuses on the passive duplicate of the living woman, on her double as an art object.

Finally, in looking back to *Laokoon*, one notices that both Hauff and Jensen break one of the rules that Lessing had derived from his study of the statue and its literary antecedents. That rule was that words are best suited to express action while a sculpture or painting is primarily restricted to represent a moment in time. However, both Hauff and especially Jensen give lengthy descriptions of the art works that play such a role on the part of the reader. Jensen, it should be noted here, had as an illustration for his novella a reproduction of "Gradiva," thus making it possible for the reader to compare it to the text. The length of the descriptions of the two art works has to be explained as being mandated by the effect the two authors want to achieve. They want the reader to be struck by the complete, or almost complete, duplication between life and art and the ensuing possibility of the transfer of the affection of the protagonist from life to art. It is probably also in connection with that desired effect that both authors chose an authentic work of art, since by doing so they increase the realism of their stories that is evident also in the many detailed observations on the physical environment within which they take place. The authentic work of art provides further evidence for the reality of the weird workings of the minds of the two protagonists and possibly of those of the readers.

Schimmang: *Intimität oder das Mädchen mit dem Perlengehänge*

Only recently did I come across a story that offered striking similarities to the two works I just discussed. Jochen Schimmang's *Intimität oder das Mädchen mit dem Perlengehänge* [Intimacy or the Girl with the Pearl Pendant] is the first of three stories of his *Königswege* [1995; Royal Paths].[5] The title of the first story refers to the well-known, enigmatic painting by Johannes Vermeer entitled "Head of a Young Girl" or "The Girl with a Pearl." A reproduction of the painting is on the dust jacket. As in the case of the Hauff and Jensen tales, Schimmang's too, has a real work of art as the central object, and he wants the reader to know the work. Vandenberg, the protagonist of *Intimität*, like Norbert in *Gradiva*, studied art. He is, at the time of the story, a professor of art history at the University of Cologne and, again like Norbert, he is attracted to an art object depicting a woman because she bears a certain resemblance to a girl he once loved. However, both protagonists have suppressed the fact that they are attracted to the respective art object for that reason. In being drawn to the woman depicted they obey a subconscious drive and are made to act in an irrational manner.

Vandenberg had many years ago loved Karin Lammers and had wanted to marry her, but he lost her as he was to lose many other women in quick succession. It was twenty years ago that he last saw Karin. At that time he began the study of art history and by now he has published a book on "Vermeer. A Study of Intimacy." When *Intimität* takes place, his book has appeared as a paperback that tourists buy when they visit the Mauritshuis, the museum in Holland that has so many Vermeer paintings. Vandenberg decides on the spur of the moment to go to Den Haag to look again at Vermeer's "Head of a Young Girl," just as Norbert had left abruptly for Pompeii. Both follow strong, irresistible urges that have to do with their unsatisfactory sex life, and neither is able to explain to himself the reason for his being dissatisfied. In Jensen's story it is the neglected girl who leads Norbert back to her, to the living woman, and thus to happiness. In *Intimität* Schimmang creates a series of parallels between Vandenberg and Vermeer, alternating the focus from one section to the other.[6] Both Vandenberg and Vermeer long for intimacy, according to the story, but love "silent" women, and both are introduced to sex by such women: a maid who wears a pearl in Vermeer's case and a woman who is an apprentice in a neighboring nursery in Vandenberg's case. While in Holland, after having spent some time in front of the Vermeer painting, he meets at a restaurant a woman who wears a pearl pendant and who turns out to have a job as a maid in the hotel in which Vandenberg is staying. She takes him to her tiny flat where Vandenberg finds fulfillment in the intimacy of the night they spend together.

Vermeer's painting shows features of Vandenberg's first love, features that he in vain had tried to find in living women for some twenty years, until his renewed study of the "Head of a Young Girl" and his chance meeting with a maid who wears a pearl pendant bring about the resolution. As in the stories by Hauff and Jensen, *Intimacy* has the protagonist give an exact description of the central art object. More than a mere description, Vandenberg presents the reader with an interpretation of Vermeer's painting of the girl in the strange costume and with the enigmatic expression of her half-open mouth and the eyes that look at you in such a haunting manner. Both his profession and his sex drive make Vandenberg look repeatedly at the painting of a woman, at Vermeer's wonderful "Head of a Young Girl." In *Intimität* Schimmang has interwoven in a masterful way the life of Vermeer and that of Vandenberg, the background for Vermeer's "Head of a Young Girl" and Vandenberg's attraction to that painting. All three authors, Hauff, Jensen, and Schimmang, have their male protagonists regard a woman as an art object and in each case a woman who looks like that work of art takes the initiative to lead the male away from his fixation with the inanimate object to the happiness with the living being.

Notes

[1] Wilhelm Hauff, *Werke*, ed. Bernhard Zeller (Frankfurt/M.: Insel, 2 vols., 1969), vol. 1, 423.

[2] Ibid., 482.

[3] Bernhard Dieterle mentions the art works in both *Die Bettlerin vom Pont des Arts* and *Gradiva*, without, however, seeing how Hauff's Cranach painting and Jensen's ancient relief become substitutes for the women the protagonists really desire. (*Erzählte Bilder,* 133–6 [*Gradiva*], 230 [*Die Bettlerin*]).

[4] The essay by Freud is most readily available in: Sigmund Freud, *Der Wahn und die Träume in W. Jensens* Gradiva *mit dem Text der Erzählung von Wilhelm Jensen,* ed. with an introduction by Bernd Urban and Johannes Cremerius (Frankfurt/M: Fischer Taschenbuch, 1973).

[5] Jochen Schimmang, *Königswege* (Frankfurt/M.: Schöffling, 1995).

[6] Except that both sections five and six as well as the last four of the twenty sections that make up the story are devoted to Vandenberg.

5: The Painting as Transgression of Time and Space Boundaries

Nossack: *Dorothea*

In chapter four we saw how the protagonist in Wilhelm Jensen's *Gradiva* transfers his affection for Zoë Bertgang to an antique relief and how Zoë then regains his affection by a daring act of duplicating the clothing of the woman depicted in the relief and by choosing the most propitious time and place for her encounters with him. There is nothing that is not rational in the duplication between relief and living character.

In the case of E. T. A. Hoffmann's *Die Fermate*, a story I will take up in the next chapter, the duplication between the scene depicted by Eduard Hummel in his "Gesellschaft in einer italienischen Lokanda" [Party at an Italian Inn] and the identical scene in the story cannot be explained easily; it is next to impossible that Hummel could have witnessed the scene in Italy when Theodor, the narrator and protagonist of the novella, happens upon the two Italian sisters in exactly the moment when the cleric, who acts as the conductor of the little concert, cuts short the fermata of one of the sisters. Hoffmann, as so often in his fiction, lets the eerie coincidence happen without offering any kind of explanation for the duplication of the scene of the painting and its repetition in the story. He is interested in the effect the various coincidences have on his characters and ultimately, of course, on his readers. The same is true of Wilhelm Hauff in *Die Bettlerin vom Pont des Arts* in which the woman depicted by Lucas Cranach, the Elder, is, according to two characters in the story, identical with a Spanish lady and her daughter both of them knew in the past. The daughter then crosses again the path of the men. Hauff gives no explanation and has no theory for this phenomenon of chronological transgression between the woman painted in the sixteenth century and the character of a story that takes place in the nineteenth.

A similar and more complex duplication between the painting of a woman and a character in a story is told in *Dorothea* (1947) by Hans Erich Nossack. The painting, it is by Karl Hofer (1878–1955), is entitled "Frau mit Kopftuch" [Woman with Head Scarf], shows a woman in a reflective attitude and wearing a housecoat that does not cover her left breast. In the novella, Dorothea, the protagonist, tells the narrator about a moment in her life when she expressed that same attitude and when she wore just that type of housecoat. The painter could not possibly have witnessed the scene; as a matter of fact, he could not have painted her at all. But in Nossack's case, in contrast to those of Hoffmann and Hauff, this irrational coincidence is evidence of a larger pattern of phenomena that the narrator claims occur especially during times of major upheavals, such as the bombing of Hamburg in July of 1943. It is clear from Nossack's life and from his other works that many of the thoughts of the narrator in *Dorothea* are reflections of the author himself who barely escaped the bombing of Hamburg where he lived at the time of the attack. This story as well as *Untergang* [Destruction], both published first in the same collection, contain many autobiographical elements. They also belong in my opinion among the most moving accounts of mass bombing of cities and the fate of the survivors.

Dorothea has a very complex structure. The narrator gives the reader the impression that he is groping to find the right approach to the events he is going to report. All of the seemingly disconnected bits and pieces deal with the issue of being at the "edge," the edge being here both a physical place like a precipice and also one where life meets with death. For the inhabitants of Hamburg the days and nights of the bombing of their city in 1943 belonged to such a time when the survivors knew that their lives had been spared by pure chance. Persons aware of the enormity of such moments, of the enormity of what it means to live at the edge, will cry out in the horror of noncomprehension if there is not someone who is near them and who can comfort them. It is Dorothea who is near Mathes, the young soldier who has survived the attack but who has lost the rest of his family. Chance has brought Mathes and Dorothea together in the desolation of the aftermath of the mass bombing, and it is he who sees to it that both of them get away from the burning, bombed out city. They make it to a nearby village where they find shelter in an unoccupied weekend bungalow. When Mathes returns that evening to the city to search for his family, he cannot even get near the street where their house once stood since the ground and the rubble is still too hot from the fire that swept over the area. Mathes realizes the full horror of the event after he has made his way back to the bungalow and tries in vain to find solace in sleep. That is when Dorothea, who is in the adjoining room, comes to his side and hushes his cry of despair.

It is against this background of horror and survival and intimacy between two strangers that a painting is introduced by the author. The narrator had gone recently to his publisher who shows his visitor a painting the publisher likes very much. It is Karl Hofer's "Frau mit Kopftuch," the painting I mentioned above. When the narrator sees it, he is astonished because he thinks he somehow knows the woman depicted. During the conversation with the publisher the narrator keeps looking at the painting. It shows a woman in a standing position, wearing a housecoat with one breast uncovered. According to the narrator, her face has the expression of someone who has suddenly stopped doing whatever she was engaged in, such as cleaning or cooking, and then asks: "Ist das das Leben?"[1] [Is that what life is all about?]. Thus, with Nossack we no longer encounter men looking at women whose beauty bewitches them, such as was the case with Turandot, the Persian story with which I began this study, but rather at ordinary women who are depicted in moments of their lives when their thoughts make them aware of the enigma of existence.

When the narrator a bit later tries to raise some cash and goes to a place in the inner city where he is told the man pays a reasonable amount for watches, he is told by Dorothea that her husband is still at work. The narrator makes it back home but, to the astonishment of his family, insists on returning to the woman's place immediately despite the almost impassable streets and the complete lack of street lights: he knows that she is the woman whom Hofer had painted. Her husband still hasn't come home. Upon the narrator's telling her about the portrait, she denies ever having posed for a painter; after all, they are not well enough off and she has never worked as a model. He doesn't dare ask any more questions about the strange coincidence but is startled to hear from Dorothea that the narrator must be the older brother of Mathes, the soldier who rescued her from the burning Hamburg, or that the narrator himself must have been her rescuer. Again and again the two try to get the other to admit that he or his younger brother was the one who saved her life and that she must have sat for Hofer's painting. But both know that they cannot be the ones involved. After some coaxing, Dorothea tells her story, interrupting herself from time to time by saying that he must know all this anyhow. He is amazed when she describes a moment when she and Mathes are in the bungalow outside of Hamburg and she puts on a blue housecoat that she has found there. She had not bothered to get dressed at the beginning of the attack and her night gown was filthy at the time. The housecoat is an old one, just like the one of the painting. Furthermore, when the narrator first met Dorothea, she wore a white head scarf identical to the one Hofer's woman wears. On his second visit he finds Dorothea in exactly the same position and with the eyes lowered as he knew her from the painting.

There is no rational explanation for the two coincidences of duplication. I said at the beginning of this chapter that the narrator and in this case also Nossack believe that such inexplicable transgressions of time and space occur in times of catastrophe when people are pushed to the edge and their minds experience feelings and thoughts that are normally kept unacknowledged. Hofer's painting of a woman in an unusual attitude and in just as unusual attire provides Nossack an important element in showing the reader how the human mind in extraordinary circumstances is connected to phenomena in which the limits of time and space are fused. At the beginning, there is the narrator's looking at the woman of Hofer's painting. He is struck by her and thinks that he knows her from somewhere. Her features, her strange posture, and her unusual attire will make him realize that Dorothea, the woman he meets in connection with his attempt to raise some cash, and Hofer's subject must be one and the same. Dorothea's story confirms what he had thought even though from a rational point of view the connection between narrator and Dorothea or that between her and Hofer cannot be explained.

Notes

[1] Hans Erich Nossack, *Interview mit dem Tode* (Berlin: Krüger, 1948), 29.

6: Seeing and Enlightenment

E. T. A. Hoffmann: *Die Fermate*

In this chapter I will discuss two rather dissimilar works, a short novella by Ernst Theodor Amadeus Hoffmann entitled *Die Fermate* and the long novel *Der Nachsommer* [1857; Indian Summer] by Adalbert Stifter. In both works a man looks at a work of art representing a woman or women and gains fundamental insights. I will take up *Die Fermate* first.

E. T. A. Hoffmann used paintings in a great number of his novels and stories. Critics relate this phenomenon to the fact that he was also a painter. It is a painting that forms an important aspect of *Die Fermate*, and as the following will show, music has an equally important role in the story. It is of course well known that Hoffmann was an accomplished composer, conductor, and music critic.

Die Fermate — the word refers to the ending of a musical piece which a singer or instrumentalist can extend according to his or her own notes or according to already prepared ones — was first published in de la Motte Fouqué's *Frauentaschenbuch für das Jahr 1816* [Pocket Book for Ladies for the Year 1816]. Hoffmann included it also in the first volume of his collection of stories, *Die Serapions-Brüder* [The Serapion Brothers] that appeared in 1819. The stories in that collection are told by various friends who gather regularly over a bottle of wine. The added introduction of the 1819 version contains a crucial remark about the meaning of *Die Fermate* that pertains precisely to the matter of this chapter, the enlightenment a man gains when looking at women depicted in a work of art, here in a painting.

The story begins with a description of an actual painting, "Die Gesellschaft in einer italienischen Lokanda" [The Party in an Italian Inn] by Johann Erdmann Hummel (1769–1852). A photo of the painting can be found at the beginning of the volume. The painting was shown at the fall 1814 exhibit of art in Berlin where, according to the story, two friends, Theodor and Eduard, see it. The scene shows two women on either side of an arbor, one singing, the other playing a guitar. A cleric acts as the conductor. There is also the innkeeper who signals a servant to be quiet while the little concert is going on. In the very center, rather far back and thus hardly visible, is a man on horseback. Standing in front of Hummel's painting with Theodor, Eduard comments on the humorous quality of the scene, but Theodor is silent, strangely attracted to the painting, and clearly disturbed by it. He looks at the painting as if he were in a dream and then accepts Eduard's suggestion to go to a nearby tavern. Even after a couple of glasses of wine Theodor keeps silent until he confesses that the painting shook him up as if he had been touched by a magic jolt. He says that by looking at the painting memories were suddenly awakened in him that were, to be sure, pleasant enough but in the strange and completely unexpected way they came alive, most disturbing. In order to explain his surprising reaction, Theodor has to tell his friend about events that go back to his childhood.

Now the actual story begins. He was poorly trained in music by second-rate, local amateurs. When he was nineteen, two Italian artists, a singer and a guitarist who also performed as a singer, came to stay for a while in the small town where Theodor lived. That was the encounter that awakened his artistic genius. He fell in love with Lauretta, the singer, and accompanied her and her sister Teresina on their concert tour by serving them as composer, pianist, and conductor. One day, at a concert, when Lauretta, who likes to indulge in virtuoso, operatic performances and to extend a note beyond its assigned measure (fermata), Theodor is bold enough to have the orchestra come in and cut short the note. She is, of course, outraged. Only Teresina's pleading keeps him from leaving the two. However, soon afterwards he overhears their condescending and disparaging remarks about himself, followed by a satirical rendition of one of his compositions. He leaves them without saying good-bye. Fourteen years later, after Theodor has become an established composer, he approaches an inn outside Rome, hears in an arbor two voices accompanied by a guitar, hears the one voice sing a long fermata that ends abruptly followed by loud cursing. A cleric runs toward Theodor and they recognize each other from the Rome musical circles. The two artists are of course Lauretta and Teresina. Theodor's successor, the cleric, had committed the same "crime" that Theodor had committed fourteen years earlier; he had cut short Lauretta's overly long fermata, which in both instances ended an aria by Anfossi. There is general recognition and reconciliation, and the two sisters try to win back Theodor but he does not follow up on their invitation to visit them in Rome.

When Theodor sees in Berlin the Hummel painting with its once beloved and admired sisters again as art objects and sees his double, the cleric, and then has time to reflect on his past involvement with the sisters, he experiences a breakthrough as to the meaning of this coincidental repetition. He now realizes that a male artist should never return to the idols of his youth since they cannot live up to the expectation he has formed. He should be forever grateful to them for having provided the spark that started his artistic development. But from then on it is essential for the artist to have the idol be creative as an internal ideal, not as something that can be approached and touched in this world. The worst the male artist could do is to marry the idealized woman since that would mean the loss of his artistic inspiration, the ruination of his artistic genius. As is well known, the above theory reflects Hoffmann's own ideas that he developed after the great disappointment of not being able to marry Julia Mark, his beautiful young piano student in Bamberg.

In the following I want to trace the way in which Theodor arrives at his insight and to pinpoint the role Hummel's painting plays in the process. There is a key passage in the introduction to *Die Fermate*, the introduction Hoffmann added when he incorporated the work in the *Serapions-Brüder*. Theodor says to his friends that he will tell them a story,

> [eine kleine Erzählung], die ich vor einiger Zeit aufschrieb und zu der mich ein Bild anregte. Sowie ich nämlich dieses Bild anschaute, wurde mir eine Bedeutung klar an die der Künstler gewiß nicht gedacht hatte, nicht hatte denken können, da Rückerinnerungen aus meinem früheren Leben auf seltsame Weise aufgingen und eben erst jene Bedeutung schufen.[1]

What Theodor is referring to here is of course the eerie coincidence — in reality created by the fiction — that Hummel depicted exactly the moment when Theodor arrived at the inn near Rome. One can assume that he identified with both the person on horseback who is hardly visible in the deep center of the painting and also — by analogy — with the cleric/conductor. But realistically it is of course impossible that Hummel could have captured on canvas that particular moment. When Theodor talks to Eduard in the tavern, he says:

> Du wirst mir aber zugestehen, daß auch heitere Erinnerungen dann den Geist gar seltsam zu erschüttern vermögen, wenn sie auf solche ganz unerwartete Weise plötzlich wie durch einen Zauberschlag geweckt, hervorspringen. Dies ist jetzt mein Fall.[2]

The painting recalls in Theodor the reunion with the sisters, but it does it in a very special way, that is, as if touched by a magic jolt. In another story, *Der Artushof* (The Court of King Arthur), which was written shortly after *Die Fermate*, Hoffmann has the narrator make this fascinating observation:

> Jener Professor *physices* meinte: der Weltgeist habe als ein wackrer Experimentalist irgendwo eine tüchtige Elektrisiermaschine gebaut, und von ihr aus liefen gar geheimnisvolle Drähte durchs Leben, die umschlichen und umgingen wir nun bestmöglichst, aber in irgendeinem Moment müßten wir darauftreten, und Blitz und Schlag führten durch unser Inneres, in dem sich nun plötzlich alles anders gestalte.[3]

My claim is that Theodor has stepped on such wires when he looks at Hummel's painting and that the result is his past is illuminated for him in a radically new way.

Up to this point Theodor had not been able to come to a resolution as to his relationship with the two sisters. They had been the ones to whom he owed his artistic awakening and ultimately his successful career as a composer. And yet, when he met with them again, he was no longer able to admire their art. The painting and the juxtaposition in his mind of the scene depicted with the abrupt ending of Lauretta's overly long fermata must have been the magic jolt that resulted in his enlightenment about his career. It now becomes clear to him that an artist has to cut through the strings that bind him or her to an admired idol. These strings are like Lauretta's fermatas in that they stretch out endlessly. What Theodor did when he had the orchestra come in and interrupt her singing was exactly the necessary thing: only in this way could he free himself from the domination of what was once his model but now had become stale and no longer inspiring. He had to go his own way. It is precisely the looking at a crucial scene from his own life in Hummel's painting that makes it possible for Theodor to gain a new understanding of himself. It is the opportunity of being able to look at that scene as a distant observer, not as someone who is an active participant. Hummel has, so to speak, objectivized the past for Theodor and thus enabled him to gain enlightenment.

But there is still more to Hoffmann's story and the way he has used Hummel's painting. The title *Die Fermata* is, to be sure, now also the title of the painting but, as Hoffmann correctly identifies it in the introductory description, the title given by Hummel is "Die Gesellschaft in einer italienischen Lokanda." The scene depicted in no way suggests the cleric's abrupt ending of the singing. Rather, in the painting he is full of admiration of Lauretta and intent so as not to miss the correct moment to lower the baton. Only in the novella does the cleric interrupt her fermata, just as Theodor had done years earlier. The title *Die Fermate* thus fits perfectly Hoffmann's story but in no way can it be applied to the scene Hummel painted. Only in the story do we have Lauretta's many fermatas, the two abrupt interruptions of these fermatas, and the ending — fermata also means the end note — of Theodor's unresolved relationship to the two sisters.

Critics have pointed to Theodor's comment in the introduction, his telling the story to his friends that Hummel's painting gave him the impetus to that story and have applied that remark to Hoffmann himself.[4] Obviously, there is merit in looking at the painting in that way. However, I hope to have shown that one must probe deeper and marvel at the creative use Hoffmann made of the scene depicted by Hummel. Hoffmann did not just recreate in the novella the scene depicted but reinterpreted it in a radical and successful way. The value of *Die Fermate* does not consist in the fact that it contains biographical details from Hoffmann's youth or that it contains the description of two types of music represented by the two sisters as one reads in various commentaries. Nor is its value the fact that Hoffman drew his initial inspiration from Hummel's painting. The story's true value lies in the fascinating way Hoffmann juxtaposes art and life and, out of a brilliant reinterpretation of the work of art, draws meaning for the protagonist and thus for every artist and also for every reader.

The structural artistry of Hoffmann's story is evident in one more respect. If we look at Hummel's painting, we notice the care with which the perspective was realized. It is no accident that he was known as "Perspektiven-Hummel." There are frames within frames: the two artists sit in the foreground, the cleric stands behind them, the innkeeper and a servant are to one side, and all five persons are under an arbor. In the center, in an opening to the sunlit outside, we see fairly far back a man on horseback. One could, as I mentioned above, identify the man with Theodor as he comes upon the scene at the Italian inn. This structure is also present in the story with Theodor as the central figure whose tale starts with two frames, each one inside the other, and whose tale also ends with the closing of the two frames.

I have devoted relatively much space to Hoffmann's short novella because of the works of German literature taken up in this study and of the many more I looked at since becoming interested in the use of works of art in literature, *Die Fermate* is the best example of the integration of a work of art into a text. Neither in the 1816 nor in the 1819 version of the text was there an accompanying reproduction of Hummel's painting. Had readers been able to compare it with the story, they might have noticed the similar framing techniques. They also might have noticed the creative reinterpretation of the scene depicted in the painting. For most readers, however, the frames in the story will help explain how Theodor gains distance from his own past. By looking at a painting that depicts the two sisters who had played a crucial role in his artistic career at exactly the moment when he crossed their path, Theodor comes to understand an essential aspect of his development as an artist.

Stifter: *Der Nachsommer*

E. T. A. Hoffmann's *Die Fermate* tells of the insight gained by the protagonist when looking at a painting that depicts a scene of his own past. As he looks at the scene, he suddenly realizes the significance of his relationship to the two women who inspired him to become an artist. In having him by pure accident come upon a painting that depicts an important event in his life, Hoffmann lets chance play a decisive role in the novella.

Adalbert Stifter in *Der Nachsommer* [1847; The Indian Summer] leaves little to chance. Among all the German novels I know *Der Nachsommer* has the most methodically worked out maturing of a person, in this case the protagonist, Heinrich Drendorf. In his development Heinrich's recognition of the beauty of the marble muse, an antique statue in the house of his mentor Risach, marks an important step. Risach sees in Heinrich at their very first meeting the qualities that cause him to decide to take on the role of mentor to the young man. Risach had already shown his ability to discover hidden excellence when he acquired a plaster statue in Italy that turned out to be a marble sculpture of unsurpassed beauty. He can, then, see beyond the surface and discover the essence of persons and objects.

As a young man Risach had been the tutor of Mathilde, the daughter of a wealthy couple. They fell in love and wanted to get married but her parents told them to wait, a condition he accepted but she couldn't. His acceptance convinced her that he didn't really love her. Thus, they had their separate loveless marriages and, after the deaths of their spouses, were granted in advanced age only an "Indian summer" of mutual affection. As Risach explains to Mathilde when they meet for the first time after the many years of separation: "Die Erklärung liegt darin, daß Du nicht zu sehen vermochtest, was zu sehen war"[5] [The explanation lies in your not being able to see what there was to see]. It is passion, according to Risach that makes one see things incorrectly. He is the person in the novel who has the most mature insight into life, nature, and art. Now, at an advanced age, they live on beautiful estates near each other, he without children, she with a daughter, Natalie, and a son. Into this "Indian summer" comes Heinrich. He was seeking shelter in Risach's house from what he believed was a threatening storm. And even though Heinrich insisted on being right about the storm and was proven wrong by Risach, the latter sees in him the qualities that make him an excellent prospect as a husband for Natalie, Mathilde's daughter.

Risach had given the sculpture, a muse from the Hellenistic period, a space by itself on the landing of the stairway of his house. The stairway is used only on special occasions; one must have a key to reach it and one must put on felt slippers when entering. The light comes from a glass dome above which makes for extraordinary effects when there is lightning and the bright light is tinged with red. The sculpture is clearly the central sacred object in Risach's house which is like a museum with its many beautifully furnished and decorated rooms in which priceless paintings hang on the walls. For Risach, though, it is essential that one recognize the sculpture's greatness. However, such recognition does not occur when first seeing it. Full appreciation comes for the select few only and then only after a process of getting to know the statue better until one day its unique beauty is revealed. In Heinrich's case love plays a significant role in that process.

Heinrich has all the advantages one could ever wish for. His family and his character belong to utopia and so do the mature Risach and Mathilde and her two children. Heinrich's parents are well-to-do, making it possible to raise their son in luxurious circumstances. He will never have to worry about earning an income. Risach sees to it that Heinrich and Natalie do not repeat the mistake he and Mathilde made when passion controlled them. Heinrich and Natalie approach each other gradually, and just as gradual is Heinrich's approach to the marble statue. He had seen Natalie in passing on a road and at a performance of *King Lear* where both were especially moved. At the time they did not know each other. In a parallel way Heinrich had passed the sculpture of the muse a few times without recognizing its greatness.

After a number of summers at Risach's house, Heinrich finds the door to the stairwell with the marble muse open. The methodical Risach who chided Heinrich on his first visit for not having replaced a book to its proper place, must have left the door open on purpose so that Heinrich would take a good look at the sculpture. It is a propitious moment since there is again, as when he first saw the statue, lightning and with each flash the white marble of the statue appears in a reddish glow.[6] The same reddish glow Heinrich sees in Natalie's face when they first meet: "Es blühte dieses Roth, wie ein sanftes Licht, auf ihren Wangen und verschönerte sie, gleichsam wie ein klarer Schimmer"[7] [This red blossomed like a soft light on her cheeks and embellished her with a clear glow]. When Heinrich saw the sculpture toward the beginning of the novel, he just noticed it, but did not react to it. Now he stops on the landing where it stands and contemplates it at great length. Nothing is there to distract him, the statue is in a space all by itself, surrounded by the gray Ammonite marble of the walls and illuminated from above. Now he can study the female figure without embarrassment, something that he could never have done when he was near Natalie, since Heinrich is, after all, the paragon of modesty and propriety. The muse's gown is a thin veil for the female body. At this juncture, just before the middle of the novel, Heinrich discovers the beauty of the marble muse: he has seen female perfection in a work of art. The transfer of that discovery to his appreciation of Natalie's beauty and perfection is automatic.[8]

When studying the statue he felt as if he were standing in front of a silent human being, and he is almost afraid the muse — interestingly enough he calls the muse here "ein Mädchen," a girl — might move at any moment.[9]

Of course, Heinrich falls in love with Natalie; at the same time his eyes are opened to the beauty of the marble muse. The sequence of events is so intertwined that one really cannot tell whether love causes his aesthetic enlightenment or whether the sudden insight into the marble muse's perfection brings about his true appreciation of Natalie's beauty. The intricate relationship between the statue and Natalie is brought out when Heinrich says that the sublime figure of the stairwell became closer and closer to him since he knew that there was something alive that resembled that figure. Ultimately, the two, Natalie and the muse, are interchangeable. The adjectives used to describe Natalie are applicable to the statue and vice versa. Both represent perfection in the value system of the novel. A remark by Risach in the course of the conversation following Heinrich's enlightenment as to the beauty of the marble muse suggests the priority of love in the sequence of events. Risach tells Heinrich that he has always believed that some strong human emotion would lead Heinrich to the discovery of the statue's greatness.[10] Risach must have meant love with that emotion.

When Heinrich discovers the muse's greatness, he is very much excited and asks Risach why he hadn't told him about the artistic value of the muse at an earlier time. Risach responds that the recognition of beauty and aesthetic greatness cannot be taught, that Heinrich's preoccupation with certain specific aspects of the natural sciences had made him unable to see the general aspects of beauty. Now that Heinrich is more of a generalist, he is able to see the statue's beauty and, by implication, Natalie's beauty.[11] In a symbolic gesture Risach gives Heinrich the key to the stairway with the marble muse and thus his blessing to proceed with the wooing of Natalie.

The ability to see correctly is, then, at the center of what characterizes the valuable person in *Der Nachsommer* and what leads to happiness. Risach's and especially Mathilde's passionate behavior prevented them from seeing things as they really were and thus thwarted their happiness when they were young. Heinrich, surrounded by good art as he is at Risach's house, is gradually led to look at art carefully and with understanding, a process that culminates in his discovery of the unsurpassed beauty of the marble muse and, at the same time, of Natalie. Thus, at the end of the novel Heinrich and Natalie are the happy young couple Risach and Mathilde failed to become. In both the aesthetic and the human realm there is gradual recognition and then the sudden bursting forth of admiration and love.

It might seem far-fetched to compare two such dissimilar texts as the short, humorous novella *Die Fermate* and the long, ponderous novel *Der Nachsommer*. But there is similarity when it comes to the male protagonist's looking at women as art objects. In both works it is the protagonist who looks at a work of art, a painting showing two women in the case of *Die Fermate*, a marble muse in that of *Der Nachsommer*. There is repetition in *Die Fermate* when Theodor's cutting short the singer's fermata is repeated by his successor years later, a scene Theodor then discovers in Hummel's genre painting. It is at that moment, as I have shown above, that Theodor gains a new understanding of himself as an artist. Heinrich also sees both Natalie and the marble muse on repeated occasions. When he has matured, there is a special moment, when looking at the muse, that he is awakened to its extraordinary beauty — and to that of Natalie. For both Theodor and Heinrich there is gradual understanding first, but then a sudden enlightenment. And in both cases the enlightenment is crucial for their development.

Notes

[1] [(a little story) that I wrote down some time ago, prompted by a painting. That is, as soon as I looked at this painting, a significance gained clarity in me of which the artist certainly did not think, could not have thought of, since memories of my early life came up in a strange way and only then created that significance.] E. T. A. Hoffmann, *Die Serapions-Brüder* (Darmstadt: Wissenschaftliche Buchgesellschaft, 1979), 56–57.

[2] [You will agree with me that even pleasant memories can shake you up in a strange manner when they in a completely unexpected way, as if awakened by a magic jolt, come upon you. That is my case now.] Ibid., 58–59.

[3] [That professor of physics had this thought: the universal spirit, being an able experimentalist, had built somewhere a strong electric generator from which mysterious wires ran across our lives. He thought that we tried as best as we could to sneak by these wires and avoid them but that at some point we had to

step on them: then a lightning bolt would blast through us reshaping us completely.] Ibid., 150.

[4] See for instance Ernst Scheyer, "Johann Erdmann Hummel und die deutsche Dichtung. Joseph von Eichendorff — E. T. A. Hoffmann — Johann Wolfgang von Goethe," *Aurora* 33 (1973), 43–62. Bernard Dieterle also discusses *Die Fermate* but in keeping with the goal of his study stresses the conversion of Hummel's scene into the story that Hoffmann has spun out of it (*Erzählte Bilder*, 66–69).

[5] Adalbert Stifter, *Sämmtliche Werke* (Prague: Calve/Reichenberg: Kraus, 1901–1939; reprint: Hildesheim: Gerstenberg, 1972), *Der Nachsommer*, vols. 6–8, ed. Kamill Eben and Franz Hüller, vol. 8, 167.

[6] Ibid., 74. See Joseph Vogl on the significance of the special light in "Der Text als Schleier. Zu Stifter's *Der Nachsommer*," *Jahrbuch der deutschen Schillergesellschaft* 37 (1993), 298–312, here 303–304.

[7] Stifter, *Sämmtliche Werke*, vol. 7, 213.

[8] This also means, as several critics have pointed out, that neither Heinrich nor Natalie have any individuality.

[9] "als ob sich das Mädchen in jedem Augenblicke regen würde," Stifter, *Sämmtliche Werke*, vol. 7, 74.

[10] "Ich habe geglaubt, irgend ein großes allgemeines menschliches Gefühl, das Euch ergreifen würde, würde Euch auf den Standpunkt führen, auf dem ich Euch jetzt sehe." [Ibid., 90; "I thought that some great, general, human emotion that would grip you would bring you to the point at which I see you now"].

[11] Most readers will go along with the words of the text and imagine indeed an extraordinarily beautiful sculpture, one of the great sculptures of the Hellenistic period. However, when looking at the actual statue that served Stifter as a model, one is less likely to agree with the words of the text. Thus, one does not know whether the photo of the statue in the Prague edition of Stifter's work is fair to the reader or to Stifter (see the reproduction between pages LXIV and LXV in vol. 6 of the edition referred to in note 5). In the same vein, some of the painters the narrator lists among those that should be considered the greatest of all times, are clearly not that great. Guido Reni is among that elite group according to several places in the text. The explanation lies of course in our changing tastes. What is irritating, though, is the claim made in the text that the aesthetic criteria presented are universal and that they should be, by implication, shared by the reader. On the other hand, the reader will welcome Roland's fascinatingly unorthodox abstract painting that is mentioned toward the end of the novel. But there is too little of such deviation from the norm. The same can be said of the account Risach gives of how his and Mathilde's courtship went awry. That relatively brief account forms a welcome relief from the all too long unfolding of the model relationship between Heinrich and Natalie.

7: Retrospective Vision: Closing the Circle

Storm: *Immensee*

The fact that I have placed Theodor Storm's *Immensee* (1850) at the end of this study will surprise many readers. The novella is not one of the great works of German literature nor does it belong among Storm's best fiction in spite of its former popularity. Its symbolism is often crude and it contains scenes that are overly sentimental. Also, the portrait of the woman I am concerned with does not seem to play a very prominent role in the story when one first reads it. However, an analysis of the place of the female portrait within the novella will show that it combines several of the functions I have discussed in previous chapters. Thus, *Immensee* is an appropriate text to take up at the end of my study.

The portrait is clearly a point of departure for the telling of the story but not in the sense that the beauty of the woman depicted will spur the beholder on to win her. There are examples of that type of interrelationship between male viewer and the portrayed female in the first chapter. In *Immensee* the woman's portrait causes Reinhard, the narrator as well as the protagonist of the inner story, to look back on his youth and his failure to win Elisabeth, the woman depicted, as his wife. Thus, the movement is both backward — Reinhard is an old man when he tells his story — and forward since he relives key scenes of their relationship as if they are in the present.

Immensee is a story with a frame, a device often used by Storm. The novella begins with Reinhard coming home one evening and telling the housekeeper to wait a while before bringing a light. We learn that Reinhard's pronunciation differs somewhat from that of the people in town, an indication that he is probably without many friends, that he is a lonely old man. The narrator mentions Reinhard's eyes first, eyes in which "his lost youth had found refuge." His eyes are described as dark and serious. As Walter Silz has so aptly observed, eloquent eyes in all their possible variations and how they look at the other person or avoid looking at that person, are among Storm's favorite devices for bringing out the nuances of the emotions his characters experience but often cannot and just as often do not want to put into words.[1] *Immensee* is certainly a prime example of that technique. When Reinhard has reached his study and has sat down in a comfortable chair, moonlight shines into the room and falls upon paintings on the wall. When the light shines upon a small painting in a simple black frame, he says softly "Elisabeth" and then comes a phrase that appears in italics: "*er war in seiner Jugend*" ["*he was in his youth*"]. What follows are eight scenes that form the inner story of the novella and run from Reinhard's and Elisabeth's childhood until she has become the wife of his friend Erich in the last scene. The novella is rounded out by a short section, entitled like the first "Der Alte" [the old man], in which we see the old Reinhard still in his chair. The moon no longer shines on Elisabeth's portrait.

The picture of the woman serves in *Immensee* as the catalyst that sets Reinhard's memory in motion and lets him visualize in detail key scenes from his youth. The young Elisabeth's face is on the wall in front of him and she is the one at the center of his memories. From the expression referred to above that "his lost youth had found refuge in his eyes," we assume from the beginning that Reinhard never achieved the happiness of a life with Elisabeth that he dreamed of first as a boy and then as a young man. The various scenes of his reminiscences will provide the explanation for Reinhard's failure to woo Elisabeth successfully.

From the first scene to the last one ("Meine Mutter hat's gewollt" — "My mother wanted it so"), it is clear that Elisabeth is very much her mother's child. The widowed mother has instilled in her daughter a concern for her mother's future who has doubts about Reinhard's ability and willingness to take care of both Elisabeth and herself. At the same time, Reinhard shows in these recreated scenes how he fails to be precise in his commitment to Elisabeth. In a key scene the two — he is seventeen and about to begin his university studies and she is twelve — get lost in the woods during a picnic. In spite of many opportunities to kiss Elisabeth and thus commit himself as the one who is going to be her husband one day, he keeps looking at her when they both sit down to rest. Later on he bases a poem on that moment in which she is celebrated as the queen of the woods with her "golden eyes." Viewing, eye contact, is, then, Reinhard's characteristic way of relating to others, both in the various scenes remembered and also when he is sitting in front of Elisabeth's portrait in the opening frame.

While at the university, Reinhard receives a letter from Elisabeth in which she mentions that upon her mother's insistence she sat for Reinhard's friend, Erich, who drew her portrait with black chalk. She hated his knowing every inch of her face, but her mother persuaded her to let Erich have his way, telling her that Reinhard's mother would be delighted to have Elisabeth's portrait as a Christmas present. We have, then, on the one hand the pattern I have described in the chapter entitled "Appropriation of the Woman by Design;" the one who paints the portrait of the woman gains a certain power over her since he has gotten to know her features in the most intimate way. On the other hand, in *Immensee* the situation is a rather confused one. To be sure, Erich will marry Elisabeth because, as I mentioned above, Reinhard has been so vague about his intentions and because her mother saw in Erich the better provider not only for her daughter but also for herself. And indeed, she will move with the young couple to the beautiful country place on the Immensee (Switzerland) that Erich has inherited from his father. But Erich is not the jealous lover who cannot stand knowing that the portrait of the beloved is not in his possession. He must even have agreed to let the portrait he made of Elisabeth be given to Reinhard's mother, thus really to a place where his rival in Elisabeth's affection, Reinhard, would see it any time he is home. The complication is, though, that Erich and Reinhard are friends, that they respect and trust each other. We have here a radically different situation from the one we observed in earlier chapters. Thus, the Prince in Lessing's *Emilia Galotti* gets Emilia's portrait not because her father, who had commissioned it and who in several way is the Prince's rival, wanted him to have the portrait. Odoardo is in all likelihood unaware of the fact that Conti, the artist, had made a copy and he is certainly unaware of the fact that Conti would show that copy to the Prince. The reader will also remember the cases, discussed in chapter two, where the artist refused to surrender the sketch he made of the woman he admired to that woman's fiancé (Dorothea Schlegel's *Florentin*, Lewald's *Jenny*, Lenz's *Die neuen Leiden des jungen W.*).

We know from the way Elisabeth responds to Reinhard's suggestion in the very first scene that they both go to far-away places that she is not the person to go against her mother's wishes. At the same time, we also know that she and Reinhard are deeply in love with each other and that he is unable to give Elisabeth his unambiguous word that he will marry her, leaving her with the vague promise that upon his return from the university "something wonderful will happen." He looks at the beloved time and time again but never gets to the point of touching her. He must have looked frequently at Elisabeth's portrait in his house and thought about the missed opportunity to have made his and her life happy. As I mentioned above, in the last encounter with Elisabeth she is Erich's wife. They have her mother with them but have no children. Elisabeth is clearly lonely, and, in spite of Erich's goodness, basically unhappy. Hauff in *Die Bettlerin vom Pont des Arts* lets the triangle end happily by freeing the mistreated wife through a divorce and getting the two who truly love each other together again. Stifter in *Der Nachsommer* has the unloved spouses conveniently die so that the two who truly love each other can still have an "Indian summer" of mutual affection. Storm is less forgiving: neither Elisabeth nor Reinhard ever achieve happiness; they will die without having been joined in their true love.

There is one more aspect of the text that pertains to Elisabeth's portrait that needs to be mentioned here. I have said that Erich's portrait of Elisabeth was to be given to Reinhard's mother. It is clear that she has died by the time the story begins, that is, the time when the elderly Reinhard sits in his study and looks at Elisabeth's portrait. The text strongly suggests that the portrait that Reinhard looks at is the chalk drawing Erich made and that Reinhard must have inherited from his mother.[2] That realization adds to our amazement: how can Reinhard keep looking at Elisabeth's portrait when that portrait was made by the man who took away the woman he — Reinhard — loved so much. We must attribute this strange behavior, that is also evident in other aspects of the relationship between Reinhard and Erich, to the friendship and respect between the two but also to a reduced level of passion in them. I say that Reinhard must have looked at Elisabeth's picture frequently because it hangs on the wall of his study where the retired old man seems to spend many hours every day. Undoubtedly, he has reminisced about his days with Elisabeth at earlier times when looking at the painting but on this particular evening he has found the right tone and the right details so as to be satisfied with the result and to be able to tell his housekeeper to bring in a light. Now he can return to the studies that occupied him as a young man, which is the study of botany.

While Storm leaves the two lovers in a state of loneliness at the end of *Immensee*, he does in my opinion grant Reinhard insight into himself, that is, into the reasons why he failed Elisabeth and thus did not achieve the happiness he hoped to share with her. Nothing is taken away from Reinhard's sense of loss at the end of the novella but as I see it, he is granted via the power of his memory the gift of clarity about himself.[3] Viewing Elisabeth as an art object, as depicted in the chalk drawing, finally permits him to see himself as an object, too: in revisiting and retelling the various scenes with Elisabeth he refers to himself in the third person and thus, like Theodor in Hoffmann's *Die Fermate*, gains distance to his past self and with that distance enlightenment. Reinhard has, while looking at Elisabeth's portrait and while seeing and re-experiencing key scenes of his youth, come to understand that he failed her by constantly having kept a distance between himself and her and that he thus lost her to his good friend who drew her portrait, the portrait which is now in front of him.

Notes

[1] Walter Silz, "Storm, *Der Schimmelreiter* (1888)," in: W. S. *Realism and Reality. Studies in the German Novelle of Poetic Realism* (Chapel Hill: U of North Carolina P, 1954), 117–36, here 135–6.

[2] Here I differ from David D. Dysart who claims that Elisabeth's portrait "is referred to once (and only within the frame)" in his *The Role of the Painting in the Works of Theodor Storm* (Frankfurt/M., etc.: Lang, 1992), 63.

[3] Raimund Belgardt also sees in the end evidence of reconciliation for Reinhard; however, he sees him an example of a poet who sacrifices Elisabeth for the sake of his art. There is no evidence for Reinhard ever having been a true poet. The studies to which he returns according to the last sentence of the novella cannot refer to his poetry, they must be the studies he took up when still young, that is, botany. Raimund Belgardt, "Dichtertum als Existenzproblem. Zur Deutung von Storm's *Immensee*," in: *Schriften der Theodor-Storm-Gesellschaft* 18 (1969), 77–88. And I agree with Eckard Pastor in denying that Reinhard has ever been a true poet. However, I differ with him when it comes to the authorship of the various episodes. Pastor claims that they are shaped by the narrator, while I take them to be reproductions of Reinhard's retrospective visions (Eckard Pastor, *Die Sprache der Erinnerung. Zu den Novellen von Theodor Storm* [Frankfurt/M.: Athenäum, 1988], 52). The phrase that immediately precedes the first episode and that I quoted toward the beginning of the chapter — *"er war in seiner Jugend"* — seems to me to indicate that what follows are Reinhard's visions and accounts, not those of a narrator. The narrator is responsible only for the short initial and concluding sections. Neither Belgardt nor Pastor mentions Elisabeth's portrait.

8: The Choice of Art Object

It seems appropriate at this point to ask how the authors of the texts taken up have selected the specific works of art. One can recognize two general types: one I will call the imagined work of art which has no equivalent in the "real" world while the other type has an equivalent in the "real" world. The texts show that most of the works mentioned here are of the former type. I will therefore discuss these first.

There is a good reason for the authors of the first chapter not to have referred to a known female portrait. One will remember that the portraits mentioned make the male viewer rush to pursue the woman depicted even if that means risking his life. Her extraordinary beauty proves irresistible. If the reader had been given an illustration or if the text had included a reference to a historically verifiable painting, the reader might very well not have been convinced that men would have been so taken by that particular woman. There would be resistance on the part of the reader to go along with the author's claim. In Lessing's tragedy *Emilia Galotti* we know by the effect Emilia has on men that she must be unusually beautiful, but each reader can and will fill in details. Thus, it would probably be wisest for a director of the play not to show her portrait to the spectators so as not to restrict their imagination. If the portrait were to be shown, it would of course have to be that of the actress playing Emilia. That brings me to the other drama I have analyzed, Schiller's *Maria Stuart*. Here Maria's portrait had propelled Mortimer's ill-fated rescue attempt. The portrait is not identified in the text as being one of the known portraits of the queen. In Schiller's play the only interference between the spectator's or reader's imagination and the Maria Stuart he or she imagines on the basis of Mortimer's reaction to her portrait is the spectator's or reader's knowledge from history that at the time of her death she was no longer the beauty of former years nor the beautiful actress on the stage as she is normally cast. But this is an issue that lies outside the area of my study. Turandot's and Pamina's (*Die Zauberflöte*) portraits basically belong to the same type.

It will also be clear that the authors of the works taken up in the chapter entitled "Possession of the Woman by Design" refer to fictional works of art. Thus, readers of Thomas Mann's *Die Bekenntnisse des Hochstaplers Felix Krull* will not look for specific models for the sketches Felix claims to have drawn of Zouzou, sketches that he was given by the Marquis de Venosta and to which Felix added a few lines to make them resemble her. The same is true of Elisabeth's portrait in Storm's *Immensee*. Had the author referred to a specific painting by a known artist, such identification would hinder the imaginative power of the reader who will in the course of reading the novella develop his or her own mental image of the woman involved. The same can be said of the various paintings of Elisabeth, the mystery gypsy in Mörike's *Maler Nolten*.

In Goethe's *Wilhelm Meisters Lehrjahre* the "Painting of the Sick Prince" is not identified in the text and thus belongs to the fictitious type of art object. Again, readers will visualize the details as they are given in the novel. Scholars have, however, found paintings of the seventeenth and eighteenth centuries that depict the exact scene described and one of the paintings comes closest to what the various characters say about it.[1] For the reader, though, that information, even looking at the painting that supposedly served as Goethe's model, adds little if anything, to the appreciation and understanding of the novel. At best, such knowledge can increase our knowledge about the creative process. Lotte's silhouette in *Die Leiden des jungen Werthers* also belongs to the fictitious type with readers coming to their own conclusion as to her appearance. The complication here lies in the fact that as so much in the novel is based on Goethe's own experiences in Wetzlar so is Lotte's silhouette. He had, as I mentioned before, cut out a silhouette of Charlotte Buff, the model for the fictional Lotte, and had taken the silhouette back to Frankfurt am Main. Again, as in the case of *Wilhelm Meisters Lehrjahre*, readers are not helped by looking at the real silhouette since their imagination is the key to an empathetic reading and since imagining Lotte's looks is an essential part of any reading in which there is emotional involvement.

I want to discuss next the Hellenistic sculpture, the marble muse, that plays such a central role in Adalbert Stifter's *Der Nachsommer*. One will recall that the narrator heaps great praise on the artistic perfection of the sculpture declaring it a truly outstanding work of art. In *Wilhelm Meisters Lehrjahre* the "Painting of the Sick Prince" was characterized by the Abbé, a connoisseur of art, as being rather second-rate, thus describing the young Wilhelm as being more interested in the subject matter of a painting than appreciative of its artistic merit. In learning that the painting is a second-rate work of art the reader who might look for the supposed model — which is certainly not one of the great works of art — will not be disappointed. The situation is different in the case of *Der Nachsommer*: when one looks at the statue Stifter must have had in mind and of which a photo is found in the Prague edition, one realizes that that statue in no way fulfills the high expectations one has when reading what both the narrator and Risach, *the* figure of authority of the novel, say about it repeatedly and with great insistence.

I have discussed in my study four texts in which the authors are most specific as to the art objects and give the artist's name (except, of course, in the case of Wilhelm Jensen's *Gradiva* where that name is unknown) the title of the work and the place where the protagonist sees it. Clearly, in each case the author wanted the readers to know that there is in reality that art work and that it would actually increase their appreciation of the story if they were to have seen it themselves. Thus, both in the case of Jensen and Nossack (second edition only) reproductions accompany the texts, and it would add to the reader's appreciation of the stories if the same were done for E. T. A. Hoffmann's *Die Fermate* and Hauff's *Die Bettlerin vom Pont des Arts*.

When we look at the four stories, Hoffmann's *Die Fermate*, Hauff's *Die Bettlerin vom Pont des Arts*, Jensen's *Gradiva*, and Nossack's *Dorothea*, we observe that the authors are intent on showing the interconnectedness between the "real" world of the reader and the world created by the text. They are especially interested in showing the weird overlapping of these two worlds. The use of works of art that the reader can verify provides excellent means to bridge the two spheres. The case of Jensen's *Gradiva* is the least relevant here since the duplication of the figure of the antique relief is, as we learn at the end of the story, the conscious effort of the girl who had been neglected by the archeologist in favor of the relief. Cleverly, Jensen withholds information about the planned duplication until the very end of the novella. Hauff in *Die Bettlerin vom Pont des Arts* gives the reader exact information about when and where the protagonist saw Lucas Cranach's painting, information that is indeed verifiable. Two men recognize their beloved in the woman portrayed, and one of them, the protagonist, meets up with her in the course of the story. Hauff never explains the coincidence that there would be the duplication of the portrait by Cranach and two women — mother and daughter — who live in the nineteenth century. As in the case of Jensen, realism has taken over at the end of the story and weird coincidences no longer form a part of that world.

In Hoffmann's *Die Fermate* such coincidences are at the heart of the novella and give evidence of the workings of forces that interconnect various aspects of our existence. Thus, Eduard Hummel's painting "Gesellschaft in einer italienischen Lokanda" has captured an incident in the protagonist's life which the artist could in all likelihood not have witnessed and, even if he had fortuitously been present, could not and did not relate to what that incident meant to the protagonist. The world as depicted in a real painting and the "real" world as presented to the reader in fiction are made to intersect in eerie ways in Hoffmann's superb craftsmanship in such an intricate manner as to shake the reader's outlook on life. The same is true of Hans Erich Nossack's *Dorothea* in which again the painter, Karl Hofer, could not have captured the Dorothea of the novella in the most unusual clothing she tells the narrator she wore at one point and in the identical posture and with the same facial expression he observed at one moment when he visited her. The duplication between the two spheres is inexplicable and forms part of a larger pattern of which Nossack sees evidence especially in times of major upheavals. It is important for him, as it was for Hoffmann, to assure the reader that he did not "invent" the painting but that it existed in the "real," verifiable world independent of the world of fiction. The coming together of these two worlds in inexplicable coincidences, worlds the reader traditionally keeps apart, characterizes both *Die Fermate* and *Dorothea* and gives them their peculiar strength. In both, the series of events has its beginning when the male protagonist looks at a painting of a woman or women that is correctly attributed in the text to a known artist.[2]

While the author who refers to a "real" art object faces the danger of having the reader disagree with what is said in the text about that object, there is the advantage for the author of being able to collapse two realms that are normally kept separate: the real world in which we live and the world as created by the author. In their stories, both Hoffmann and Nossack have exploited that possibility with great success, and in both stories the point of departure is the narrator's looking at the painting of a woman or women.

Notes

[1] See chapter III, note 1.

[2] Interestingly enough, while the first edition of the collection of stories within which *Dorothea* appeared was entitled *Interview mit dem Tode*, the second has the title *Dorothea. Berichte* (1948). The change of title clearly indicates Nossack's own high evaluation of *Dorothea*. Also, in the second edition Karl Hofer's "Frau mit Kopftuch" [Woman with Head Scarf] was reproduced on the dust jacket. The painting is identified on the back of the title page. Also reproduced on the dust jacket is Vermeer's "Head of a Young Girl" in Jochen Schimmang's *Königswege. Intimität*, the first story in the collection, a story in which Vermeer's painting plays a crucial role, I discussed in chapter IV.

Conclusion

My readings of a variety of German literary works since the eighteenth century have focused on the occurrence in these texts of men looking at art that represents women. The frequency of the phenomenon is undoubtedly due in part to the fact that most of the works included were written by men. But even in the two novels discussed here that were written by women, men were doing the looking. Thus, my findings confirm what is generally known and has been studied and reported on by social psychologists: men like to look at women. Of course, the social psychologists base their results on actual situations while I have dealt with the phenomenon only in literature.

The variety of ways in which authors relate certain characters to art works depicting women is truly astonishing. Establishing common denominators within the great variety has been the principle determining individual chapters. While, with the exception of one transposition in chapter two where I discussed, for obvious reasons, Plenzdorf's *Die neuen Leiden des jungen W.* right after Goethe's *Die Leiden des jungen Werthers*, a chronological order as to the works discussed was followed within each chapter. On the other hand, the sequence of chapters was established on the basis of how the men looking at the woman or women portrayed reacted to the work of art.

One could say that any object mentioned by an author can yield such a multiplicity of interrelationships among characters and that object. Thus, Hermann J. Weigand, the teacher to whom I owe most of whatever insight into works of literature I developed, has shown the masterful ways in which Thomas Mann uses chairs in *Der Zauberberg*.[1] Depictions of women pose a special challenge since the author has to deal with the product of another artist as well as with the duplicate characters in the texts. Many of the men in the works studied desire to have either the woman of flesh and blood or the artistic duplicate or want to have both. Several texts show how the possession of the woman's portrait seemed to give its owner a certain control over the person depicted. In some cases the man had to be content with the lifeless duplicate which he could scrutinize at his leisure, making "her" the passive object of his desire which the living person would not be. In such a situation one could speak of the phenomenon of voyeurism as characterizing the man's approach to the woman. In an extreme case, in Goethe's parody *Der Triumph der Empfindsamkeit* the man, the butt of the parody, actually prefers the dummy to the real person. Goethe is clearly prioritizing life over art, as he did in *Werther* where the protagonist had in his possession the silhouette he had made of Lotte but found that it was not a satisfactory substitute for the real person.

My study belongs in a wider sense to the way men see and approach women. It is well known and born out by the texts analyzed here that there are certain constants characterizing the man/woman relationship, at least since the eighteenth century. Nobody today, seeing a performance of *Emilia Galotti* or reading the drama, will question the Prince's feeling of rapture when he is shown Emilia's portrait nor his irresistible urge to be close to her, to want to have her. Nor will we doubt Tamino's falling in love with Pamina in *Die Zauberflöte* on the basis of his having looked at her portrait and then going off to rescue her from her supposed abductor. Every reader knows that portraits preserve strong memories of the persons depicted as we witness in Storm's *Immensee*. Also, we know that art objects in general and those depicting human beings in particular can have an impact on our life. Rilke's "Du mußt dein Leben ändern" [You must change your life], the last sentence of "Archaischer Torso Apollos" comes to mind here.

My goal has not been an analysis of the art works selected by an author, even in those cases where we can identify these works. There already exists a number of studies on the probable prototype for the "Bild vom kranken Königssohn," the painting Goethe used in *Wilhelm Meisters Lehrjahre* as well as studies on Goethe's views of the arts. In each case in which an author used a "real" work of art such inquiries could have been pursued. They would, though, not have furthered the goal of this study, that is, the uncovering of the many ways in which authors have made men viewing women as art objects an integral part of their works.

Of all the examples I have discussed two stand out in my view as yielding especially valuable insights into the process of how an author changes an ordinary object into one of special meaning within the text. First, the creative process is clearly evident in Hoffmann's *Die Fermate*. He reinterprets Johann Erdmann Hummel's genre piece "Gesellschaft in einer italienischen Lokanda" as a scene in which the cleric, who will serve in the story as the protagonist's double, cuts short the fermata of the singer. The theme of interruption will be at the center of the meaning of the novella. Second, for his *Dorothea* Nossack saw in Karl Hofer's "Frau mit Kopftuch" the portrait of a woman he calls Dorothea as captured by the painter in a pensive moment after the bombing of Hamburg, a woman who becomes a "gift of God" to her devastated rescuer. Dorothea firmly believes that he is either the narrator himself or at least his younger brother even though this is realistically an impossibility. Living at the edge where time and space become blurred is the theme of the novella.

It is the uncovering of the intricate patterns and significations created by the author between an art work depicting women and various male characters that has been the goal of my study. I believe that studying texts that reveal similar patterns allows for interesting comparisons and, most important, for new insights into the texts selected.

Notes

[1] Hermann J. Weigand, *The Magic Mountain. A Study of Thomas Mann's Novel 'Der Zauberberg'* (Chapel Hill: U of North Carolina P, 1964), 80–81.

Select Bibliography

Editions

Freud, Sigmund. *Der Wahn und die Träume in W. Jensens "Gradiva" mit dem Text der Erzählung von Wilhelm Jensen*, ed. with an introduction by Bernd Urban and Johannes Cremerius (Frankfurt/M.: Fischer Taschenbuch, 1973).

Hauff, Wilhelm. *Werke*, ed. Bernhard Zeller (Frankfurt/M.: Insel, 2 vols., 1969).

Hoffmann, E. T. A. *Die Serapions-Brüder*. (Darmstadt: Wissenschaftliche Buchgesellschaft, 1979).

Goethe, Johann Wolfgang von. *Wilhelm Meisters Lehrjahre*. In: *Sämtliche Werke, Briefe, Tagebücher und Gespräche*, sec. I, vol. 9 (Frankfurt/M.: Deutscher Klassiker Verlag, 1992).

Lenz, Jakob Michael Reinhold. *Werke und Briefe in drei Bänden*, ed. Sigrid Damm (Munich: Hanser, 1987).

Lewald, Fanny. *Jenny. Historischer Roman*. (Berlin: Der Morgen, 1967).

Mörike, Eduard. *Maler Nolten*. In: *Werke und Briefe*, vol. 3 (Stuttgart: Klett, 1967).

Nizami. *The Story of the Seven Princesses*. (London: Bruno Cassirer, 1976).

Nossack, Hans Erich. *Interview mit dem Tode*. (Berlin: Krüger, 1948).

Schikaneder, Emanuel, *Die Zauberflöte*. In: *Deutsche Literatur. Reihe Barock*, vol. 1, *Die Maschinenkomödie*, ed. Otto Rommel (Leipzig: Reclam, 1935), 263–318.

Schimmang, Jochen. *Intimität oder das Mädchen mit dem Perlengehänge*. In: J. S. *Königswege* (Frankfurt/M.: Schöffling, 1995), 9–96.

Schlegel, Dorothea. *Florentin. Ein Roman. Herausgegeben von Friedrich Schlegel*, vol. 1, ed. Paul Kluckohn. In: *Deutsche Literatur. Reihe Romantik*, vol. 7 (Leipzig: Reclam, 1933) 89–237.

Stifter, Adalbert. *Der Nachsommer*. In: *Sämmtliche Werke*, vols. 6–8, ed. Kamill Eben and Franz Hüller (Prague, 1916–1921; reprint: Hildesheim: Gerstenberg, 1972).

Secondary Literature

Dieterle, Bernard. *Erzählte Bilder. Zum narrativen Umgang mit Gemälden.* (Marburg: Hitzeroth, 1988).

Freedberg, David. *The Power of Images. Studies in the History and Theory of Response.* (Chicago and London: U of Chicago P, 1989).

Haslinger, Adolf. "'Dies Bildnisz ist bezaubernd schön.' Zum Thema 'Motiv und epische Struktur' im höfischen Roman des Barock," *Literaturwissenschaftliches Jahrbuch*, NF, 9 (1968), 83–140.

Weisstein, Ulrich. "Literature and the Visual Arts." *Interrelations of Literature*, ed. By Jean-Pierre Barricelli and Joseph Gibaldi (New York: The Modern Language Association of America, 1982), 251–77.

Index

Ammerlahn, Hellmut 41 n.10
Andrews, Dana xii
Anfossi, Pasquale 74
Antiochus 44
arousal 12, 13, 22 n.8

Becker, Jurek 21 n.3
Belgardt, Raimund 88 n.3
Bendemann, Eduard 35, 36
Bürgel, J. Christoph 21 n.2
Buss, David M. 3, 4 n.1

Cranach, Lucas, the Elder 57, 58, 59, 60, 62, 63, 66 n.3, 68, 92

Daly, Martin 10, 21 n.6
delusion 57, 60, 61, 62
development 13–14, 20, 45, 77, 81
Demetrius 44
Dieterle, Bernard xii, xiv n.4, 56 n.6, 66 n.3, 82 n.4
Don Juan 40
double 50, 52, 55, 57, 63, 64, 74, 97
dummy 31, 32, 40, 96
Dysart, David L. 88 n.2

enlightenment 72, 74, 75, 76, 80, 81, 87
epiphany 46

fate 46, 52–54
fetishism 63
Fischer, Petra 22 n.11
fixation 63, 66

Flax, Neill 10, 21–22 n.8
foreshadowing 45, 49, 50–55
Fouqué, Friedrich von, Baron de la Motte 72
frame 76–77, 83
Freedberg, David 13, 22 n.10
Freemasons 13
Frenzel, Elisabeth 21 n.2
Freud, Sigmund 47, 61, 67 n.4

Goethe, Johann Wolfgang von xi, 23–26, 27, 28, 29–31, 32, 35, 36, 37, 39, 40, 41 n.5 and 6, 44–49, 51, 53–54, 55, 90, 91, 95, 96

Haslinger, Adolf xii, xiv n.3
Hauff, Wilhelm 5, 20 n.1, 57–61, 63, 64, 66, 66 n.1 and 3, 68, 69, 86, 91–92
Helen of Troy 3, 18
Héloise 15
Hofer, Karl 69, 70, 71, 92, 93 n.2, 97
Hoffman, Ernst Theodor Amadeus 57, 68, 69, 72–77, 81, 81, n.1, 87, 91, 92–93, 97
Homer 2, 3, 18
Hummel, Johann Erdmann 68, 72–77, 92, 97
humor 14, 48, 63

imagination 2, 15, 48–49, 89, 90
integration 44, 66, 77, 96
interference 18, 19, 89, 90, 91

Jensen, Wilhelm 57, 61–64, 66, 66 n.3, 68, 91, 92
Jesuits 16
Jews 35, 36, 37

Lange-Kirchheim, Astrid 41 n.6
Laocoon 1–3, 10, 18, 19, 20, 44, 48–49, 51, 64
Lenz, Jakob Michael Reinhold 23, 25–28, 29, 31, 37, 39, 40, 41 n.3 and 5, 85
Lesser, Wendy xii, xiv n.5
Lessing, Gotthold Ephraim 1–3, 8–11, 12, 14, 15, 18, 19, 20, 23, 24, 34, 35, 36–37, 44, 48, 51, 64, 85, 89, 96
Lewald, Fanny 35–37, 39, 40, 42 n.10, 85

Madonna 15
Mann, Thomas 37–41, 90, 95
man's gaze 3, 55, 63, 64
Mark, Julia 74
McCarthy, Mary xi–xii, 9–10, 38–39, 43 n.11
McPherson, Mark xii
memory 37, 73, 84, 86, 87, 96
Mörike, Eduard 46, 49–55, 56 n.8 and 9, 90
Mozart, Wolfgang Amadeus 11–14, 17, 18, 19, 20, 89, 96

Nizami xi, 5–7, 11, 17, 18, 19, 20, 21 n.2, 70, 89
Nossack, Hans Erich 68–71, 71 n.1, 91, 92–93, 93 n.2, 97

painting as psychological test 14, 15
Pastor, Eckart 88 n.3
perspective 76–77
picaresque novel 39
Plenzdorf, Ulrich 28–29, 34, 40, 95
Plutarch 44
Poe, Edgar Allan 23
pregnant moment 2
Preminger, Otto xii
Prutti, Brigitte 21 n.5 and 7, 21–22 n.8, 23

rape 13, 18
realism 52–54, 57–58, 64
repression 62, 65
Reni, Guido 82 n.11
Rilke, Rainer Maria 96
romanticism 57

Saine, Thomas P. 41 n.2, 47, 56 n.5
Samaritan 46
Sammons, Jeffrey L. 56 n.7
Scheyer, Ernst 82 n.4
Schikaneder 11–14, 17, 18, 19, 20, 89, 96
Schiller, Friedrich 5, 8, 14–20, 32, 89
Schimmang, Jochen 65–66, 67 n.5, 93 n.2
Schlegel, Dorothea 32–35, 36, 37, 40, 42 n.7, 85
Schweitzer, Christoph E. xiv n.1, 56 n.2
Scott, Sir Walter 35, 37
Seleucus I 44
sentimentality 29–31, 40
Shakespeare, William 24, 79
Silz, Walter 83–84, 88 n.1
Stifter, Adalbert 72, 77–81, 82 n.5, 86, 90–91
stoicism 1
Storm, Theodor 37, 83–87, 90, 96

Stratonike 44

tableau vivant 22 n.8, 35–37
talisman 26
Tierney, Gene xii
transfer 57, 60, 61, 63, 64, 68, 79
Turandot xi, 5–7, 11, 17, 18, 19, 20, 21 n.2, 70, 89
Tussaud, Marie Gresholtz 30

Venus 15
Vermeer, Johannes 65–66, 93 n.2
Vogl, Joseph 83 n.6
voyeurism 96

Weigand, Herman J. 95, 97 n.1
Weisstein, Ulrich xi, xiv n.2
Wieland, Christoph Martin 11
Wilson, Margo 10, 21 n.6
Winckelmann, Johann Joachim 1
woman as possession 7, 9, 10, 18, 32, 34
woman as sorceress 9, 12, 70
work of art as duplicate 25, 27, 30, 31, 32, 40, 61, 62, 63, 64, 68, 70–71, 91, 95, 96
work of art as substitute 23, 24, 26, 27, 29, 37, 59, 60, 61